RAG RUGS,
PILLOWS, & MORE

RAG RUGS, PILLOWS, & MORE

over 30 ways to upcycle fabric
for the home

Elspeth Jackson

CICO BOOKS
LONDON NEW YORK

For my mum.

Published in 2016 by CICO Books
An imprint of Ryland Peters & Small Ltd

20–21 Jockey's Fields,   341 E 116th St,
London   New York,
WC1R 4BW   NY 10029

www.rylandpeters.com

10 9 8 7 6 5 4 3 2 1

A CIP catalog record for this book is available
from the Library of Congress and the British
Library.

ISBN: 978 1 78249 363 1
Printed in China

Editor: Gillian Haslam
Designer: Geoff Borin
Photographer: Emma Mitchell
Stylist: Nel Haynes
Illustrator: Harriet de Winton

Art director: Sally Powell
Production controller: David Hearn
Publishing manager: Penny Craig
Publisher: Cindy Richards

All instructions in this book contain both
standard (imperial) and metric measurements.
Please use only one set of measurements, as they
are not interchangeable.

CONTENTS

INTRODUCTION

Are you a creative crafter looking to try something new? Have you wanted to give rag rugging a go for a while but didn't know where to start? Do you have a treasure trove of fabric offcuts and old clothing that you'd love to turn into something beautiful?

If you answered "yes" to any of those questions, then chances are that this is the right book for you. Here you will learn how to create rag rug masterpieces using just a few basic tools and recycled fabric and clothing.

Starting with the basics, you will first learn about the tools of rag rugging, how to use them, and how to prepare your burlap/hessian and fabric strips. You will then master the three main rag rugging techniques—loopy, shaggy, and braided—and learn how to apply them to a range of great projects.

As with anything, the best way to improve is with practice and, with over 30 rag rug projects to choose from, there are plenty of options to help you hone your skills. The projects range in level from simple starter projects, such as my Teatime Trivet on page 84 (which is perfect for beginners to try both the loopy and shaggy techniques), to more challenging and intricate pieces, like the Folk Art Wall Hanging on page 80. I recommend starting with a small piece so you can finesse your technique, but rag rugging is a pretty simple craft so after a little practice you'll be ready to take on a whole rag rug.

The techniques and step-by-step instructions for the projects are accompanied by simple, color illustrations to show you how things should look. There is also a handy design section where I share my best tips and tricks, picked up over years of rag rugging. By the end of this book, you will have the skills and confidence needed to create your very own rag rug designs and projects. How great is that?

WHY IS RAG RUGGING SO WONDERFUL?

Rag rugging is the ultimate simple, yet sustainable craft. The basic equipment is relatively cheap and easy to buy. What's more, finding the fabric to work with is as easy as sorting through your closet for something you haven't worn for a few years (it's useful for decluttering, too!). The techniques are simple to learn

and hard to forget, as they involve a lot of repetition. This means that once you get going, you can even rag rug while watching TV.

SO WHERE DO I COME IN?

Rag rugging has existed in some form since the eighteenth century, but it has fluctuated in popularity over the years. When I first became interested in the craft in the noughties it was not particularly widespread, and any designs I came across tended to be dark and a bit dated. Rugs were the only rag projects out there and there seemed to be very little innovation going on in the craft.

As with most people learning a new craft, at first I just wanted to make beautiful, personalized pieces for myself, but I soon realized that I wanted to do something much bigger. I wanted to bring rag rugging into the twenty-first century with fresh, modern designs, and inspire other rag ruggers to experiment. Rag rug is a form of textile after all, so why couldn't it be used for more than just rugs? Well, my designs and products turned out to be so popular that in 2014 I left my job to start my very own rag rug business, "Ragged Life" (www.ragged-life.com). I've been making rag rug commissions, running rag rug workshops, and selling rag rug kits ever since.

But enough about me—it's time for you to get started!

Elspeth Jackson

TOOLS AND EQUIPMENT

BASIC EQUIPMENT

The tools I use for rag rugging are a latch hook and a rag rug spring tool. Other rag rug tools do exist, but the main tool used in this book is the latch hook. I find it the simplest and most versatile tool for beginners to use.

LATCH HOOK

With the latch hook you work from the front of the burlap/hessian, so you can see exactly how your rag rugging is looking as you do it. This means that if you feel something doesn't look quite right, you can adjust it there and then with little effort.

Some latch hooks have wooden handles and some have plastic. They all do the job, but it is a matter of personal preference which one you choose. I always use a wooden-handled latch hook because it feels more natural and fitting with the ethos of rag rugging, but use whatever feels best for you.

All latch hooks have a deep hook to pick up the strips of fabric and a little metal "latch" to secure them in place. Some people find that they

rag rug faster without the latch. If at any stage the latch is causing problems for you, tape the latch open or remove it entirely. See pages 18–21 for how to use this tool.

I'm often asked whether a crochet hook can be used instead of a latch hook. Unfortunately, the simple answer is "no." The groove of a crochet hook is too shallow to cradle the strips properly and prevent them from falling off.

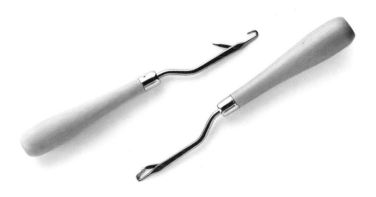

BURLAP/HESSIAN

The traditional base for rag rugs is called either burlap or hessian, depending on where you come from in the world. It is exactly the same material whatever name it is sold under. Historically, burlap was used as the base material for rag rugs as it was commonly available (old sacking was repurposed) and extremely strong. Rag rugs made using burlap last for years and years and you can still see many Victorian rag rugs made on a burlap base in museums and country homes.

Burlap comes in a number of forms and there are a couple of things to look out for when buying it.

Weave: The weave of the burlap is the most important factor. If the weave is too tight, it is really difficult to pull the strips of fabric through, but if the weave is too loose the rags won't stay in securely. Unfortunately, burlap hasn't been standardized in terms of weight and weave, so buying the right type for rag rugging can be a bit tricky. Below is a life-size photo of the weave I recommend. You can choose burlap that is slightly looser than this, but I wouldn't use anything tighter. There are roughly 4–5 holes per ½ in (1 cm).

Quality: It is important that you invest in good-quality burlap as it will make the rag rugging much more pleasant. A little bit of variation in the burlap is to be expected as it is a natural product, but avoid using burlap that has an uneven weave or is "hairy."

Where possible, I advise buying burlap in person or from one of the stockists on page 127, as it is very difficult to judge the quality and weave of burlap purely from pictures on the internet. To help you buy the correct weave, I recommend taking this book and a ruler with you to the store.

Below: The best burlap has 4–5 holes per ½ in (4 holes per 1 cm).

GAUGE

A rag rug gauge is a timesaving tool that aids and speeds up the process of cutting strips to the correct length for shaggy rag rugging. When buying a gauge, make sure that the groove is wide and deep enough to fit the blades of your fabric scissors comfortably. Although vintage gauges look great, they are usually made for wool latch hooking, as opposed to rag rugging, so are slightly the wrong size. I recommend buying a specific rag rug gauge where possible. See page 15 for how to use this tool.

RAG RUG SPRING TOOL

The rag rug spring tool is a tool that can be used for shaggy rag rugging. It is particularly useful for joining pieces of burlap together where you do not have access to the underside of the hessian (for example, in the Deep Blue Pouffe on page 66). Only a couple of projects in this book require the use of a rag rug spring tool, so don't worry if you do not own one. See page 22 for how to use this tool.

FABRIC SCISSORS

Rag rugging involves a fair amount of cutting of fabric, so having a good pair of fabric scissors is essential. Just remember not to cut anything other than fabric with them (especially not burlap), as this blunts the blades.

EVERYDAY SCISSORS

For most of the projects, you will need a second pair of scissors to cut the burlap and other materials.

FABRIC

Any fabric can be used for rag rugging, regardless of the material, pattern, or state it is in. However, some fabrics are easier to use than others—see pages 25–26.

OTHER EQUIPMENT

FOAMBOARD, SCALPEL, AND CUTTING MAT

Foamboard is a great, solid base for decorative rag rug projects. I recommend using ¼ in (5 mm) thick foamboard, as it is sturdy without adding unnecessary bulk. Foamboard is notoriously difficult to cut—scissors struggle to make a dent in it—so the only way to cut it is using a sharp scalpel on a cutting mat. When cutting with a scalpel, be extremely careful to keep your fingers and thumbs out of the way and use a metal ruler to cut along straight lines where possible. If the scalpel isn't passing through the foamboard smoothly, replacing the blade can help.

As an alternative to foamboard, you can use layers of cardboard instead. Keep stacking layers and gluing them together until the cardboard reaches ¼ in (5 mm) in thickness.

FRAME/LARGE EMBROIDERY HOOP

I'm often asked whether you need to use a frame to rag rug. When using a latch hook, it isn't necessary. In fact, I never use a frame and none of the projects in this book require one. If you do decide to try out a frame, for smaller pieces of rag rugging an embroidery hoop can be used as a cheap alternative to buying a full-size frame.

GLUE GUN

Some projects require the use of a glue gun for finishing touches. Glue guns can now be bought cheaply in store or online. There is no need to buy an expensive model, as none of my projects require large amounts of gluing. It is, however, useful to buy transparent glue sticks so that the glue is less visible in your work.

MARKER PEN

You can use any thick marker pen to sketch onto burlap. It doesn't matter if you use permanent or washable ink. Any markings will be covered with rag rugging, so choose a color that is clearly visible on the burlap.

ROTARY CUTTER, CUTTING MAT, AND RULER

If you have these three pieces of equipment, they can be used as an alternative to fabric scissors to cut strips of material for rag rugging. See the method on page 16.

SEWING MACHINE/NEEDLE AND THREAD

To hem burlap, a sewing machine can save a lot of time. Your machine only needs two stitches—a simple running stitch and a zig zag stitch. If you do not have a sewing machine, you can hem by hand. See instructions for both methods on pages 11–12.

STAPLE GUN/THUMBTACKS

For many of these projects you will need a staple gun to secure your rag rug piece to a firm base. If you don't have one thumbtacks/drawing pins or strong glue can usually be used as an alternative. The type of staple gun does not matter, but I use ½-in (10-mm) deep staples.

TAPE MEASURE/RULER

Use a tape measure or ruler if you want to follow my step-by-step instructions precisely. When measuring the circumference of objects (for example in the Odds and Ends Containers on page 95), it is easiest to use a flexible tape measure as it can bend. If you do not have one, you can use string and a rigid tape measure instead. For this method, see the Deep Blue Pouffe on page 66.

RUG CANVAS

I usually recommend a burlap base for rag rug projects, but for every rule there's an exception. Denim is a particularly difficult fabric to rag rug with and takes its toll on the base material. Rug canvas generally has a looser weave, so the thick denim strips can fit through, and it is more rigid than burlap, so it makes a much firmer base. I don't recommend using rug canvas unless you have to, as it cannot be put in the washing machine. See the Denim Chevron Rug on page 39 (and shown below) to see how I used rug canvas.

TECHNIQUES

WORKING IN STRAIGHT LINES

With some projects, you begin by sketching your design directly onto the burlap/hessian. However, burlap is an organic product that doesn't always play by the rules. Sometimes you think you have sketched a straight line, but soon find out that it isn't quite as straight as you thought. This technique ensures that your lines are truly straight and that the rug you're planning isn't going to taper out from one end to the other.

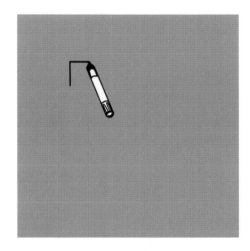

1 Using a marker pen, mark one of the corners of the square or rectangle on the burlap. Make sure you've positioned this corner so that there is enough space for the square or rectangle to fit onto the burlap.

2 Remove the vertical burlap strand at the marked corner by following the burlap strand you have drawn on top of to the frayed edge of the burlap and gently pulling it out. The burlap will bunch up as you do this, but do not worry. If the edge of the burlap is a selvage/selvedge or already hemmed, you may need to make a small cut at the end of the strand so that it will come out. Pulling out the strand creates a gap in the burlap. This gap is in line with the weave and as straight a line as you will achieve. Use the same method to pull out the horizontal burlap strand at the corner.

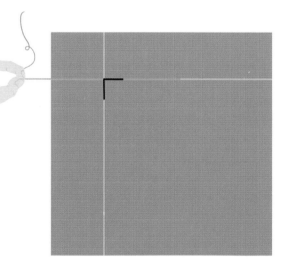

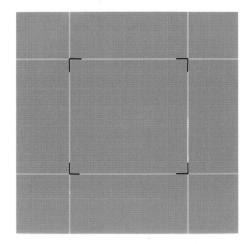

3 Measure from your first corner along the gaps left by the missing strands and mark out the other corners of the square or rectangle. Pull out the vertical and horizontal strands at these corners to create an "invisible" square or rectangle. When you hem, use these gaps as guides to keep in line with the weave of the burlap.

HEMMING BURLAP

Burlap/hessian is usually sold by the yard or meter and cut from a large roll. This means that your piece will probably have two selvage/selvedge edges and at least two sides that are raw or cut. Rag rugging close to a cut edge will cause the burlap to unravel and any fabric pieces to fall out.

Hemming the burlap before you start rag rugging will protect your work. You do not need to hem selvage edges. There are two types of hemming used in this book—edge hemming and placeholder hemming. Edge hemming is the super-secure method used for the edge of rugs and wall hangings, as it will withstand a lot of wear and tear. Placeholder hemming is used to keep the burlap intact long enough for you to rag rug your piece and assemble it. It is traditionally used for decorative pieces such as wreaths and pillows, where there are further steps to assemble the project after the rag rugging is complete.

EDGE HEMMING

This can be done either by hand sewing or machine stitching. Using a sewing machine is the faster option.

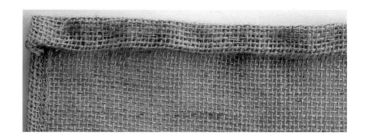

EDGE HEMMING BY HAND

1 Mark out your design on the burlap. If your design is a square or rectangle, first follow the "working in straight lines" method (see left) to ensure that the edges of your design are in line with the weave of the burlap. If your design has to be a precise size, add ¾ in (2 cm) to the measurements for each edge that will be hemmed (as the hemming will reduce the finished size of the rug). Cut out the burlap so that the edges are clean cut without any loose threads.

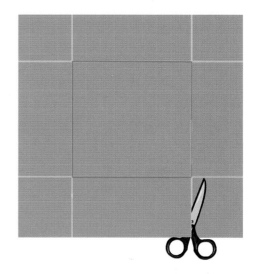

2 Fold your first edge over by ½ in (1 cm), then fold it over again by ½ in (1 cm) to trap the frayed edge of the burlap underneath. Pin the edge in place.

TIP

TO MAKE YOUR HEMMING EVEN MORE ROBUST, RAG RUG THROUGH THE HEM ITSELF WHEN MAKING YOUR PROJECT. RAG RUGGING THROUGH MULTIPLE LAYERS CAN BE QUITE DIFFICULT, BUT USING THE SHARP END OF THE LATCH HOOK TO ENLARGE THE HOLES CAN HELP.

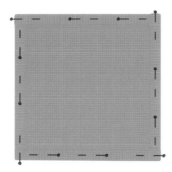

3 Repeat step 2 for each edge of the burlap to be hemmed. Corners can be quite tricky to pin as they are bulky.

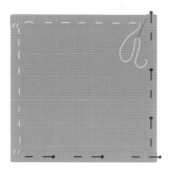

4 Baste/tack along each of the hems of the rug, close to the inner fold. Sew a few stitches into each corner as you go to make them more secure. I use button thread for extra strength.

EDGE HEMMING BY MACHINE

1 Mark out your project on the burlap. If your design is a square or rectangle, first follow the "working in straight lines" method (see page 10) to ensure that the edges of your design are in line with the weave of the burlap. If your design has to be a precise size, add ½ in (1 cm) to the measurements for each edge that will be hemmed.

2 Zig zag stitch along the marked-out piece. Keep your stitch length at its default setting (mine is 2.0), but adjust your stitch width to its widest setting (my sewing machine goes up to 6.0). This will ensure that both the horizontal and vertical strands of the burlap are caught by the machined stitches. Keeping as close as possible to the stitching but without snipping it, cut around the outside of the zig zag hemming.

3 Fold the first edge over by ½ in (1 cm) and pin in place. Repeat for each edge of the burlap you would like to hem. You will need to overlap the corners.

4 Sew a running stitch along each of the hems to secure in place, sewing just inside the zig zag hemming. The stitch length does not matter.

TIP

IF YOU ARE MAKING A SHAGGY RAG RUGGED PROJECT, YOU WILL NOT NEED TO RAG RUG THROUGH THE HEM AS IT IS NARROW AND WILL BE OBSCURED BY THE FABRIC STRIPS. FOR LOOPY PROJECTS, TRY TO RAG RUG THROUGH THE HEMMING ITSELF OR THE BURLAP WILL SHOW.

PLACEHOLDER HEMMING

Placeholder hemming is a less secure form of hemming used only for projects that require further assembling after they are fully rag rugged. Depending on the type of project, you may need either one or two rows of placeholder hemming (the instructions for each project will make this clear). The number of rows is determined by the rag rugging technique, the size of the project, and the way it is assembled. Some projects also require two rows of placeholder hemming stitch on top of each other for extra security.

1 Leaving at least 2 in (5 cm) between the frayed edge of the burlap and your design, draw your project on the burlap. If your design is a square or rectangle, first follow the "working in straight lines" method (see page 10) to ensure that the edges of your design are in line with the weave of the burlap.

2 Adjust the settings on your sewing machine so that the stitch width is at its widest setting (mine goes up to 6.0) and your stitch length is at its default setting (mine is 2.0). Zig zag stitch around the piece.

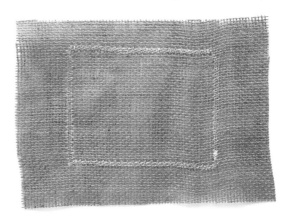

PREPARING YOUR FABRICS

Any kind of fabric can be used for rag rugging—bed linen, old clothing, fabric offcuts from other craft projects, etc. However, all fabrics must first be cut into strips about ¾ in (2 cm) wide and, initially, as long as possible. I always try to get as many strips out of one garment as possible. If you are using recycled clothing or offcuts, once you have run out of a fabric it is nearly impossible to find the same fabric again (particularly with patterned materials). Being clever with your cutting also avoids wastage.

Preparing the fabric is one of the most time-consuming parts of rag rugging, so here are my tried-and-true tips on how to turn items of clothing into strips quickly.

CUTTING STRIPS WITH SCISSORS

It is important to use a sharp pair of fabric scissors, as you will be cutting through multiple layers of fabric at a time. Dressmaking scissors can be used with most fabrics. However, tougher materials, such as denim, can blunt them—so if your scissors are your pride and joy, it may be a worth investing in another pair. Don't worry about cutting strips completely straight, as little kinks won't show up in your rag rugging.

1 Choose the material to cut up—I recommend practicing with an old t-shirt first. Turn the item inside out so that any seams are visible. Cut along one edge of every seam, except the bottom hem and neckline, to separate the garment into its constituent pieces. For a t-shirt you will usually have four sections—front, back, and two arms. All the seams should be left on at this stage.

2 I use fabric seams in my rag rugging to add texture and avoid wastage. Always cut along the line of seams, never horizontally across them. Cut strips ½ in (1 cm) away from the stitching of the seams. Strips containing seams are cut slightly narrower than usual to compensate for the added thickness of the stitching. Cut off and discard any parts of the t-shirt that cannot be used, such as stiff or thick collars and clothing labels. If you have any "lumps" at the end of your strips where two seams met, cut these off as they will show up in your rag rugging.

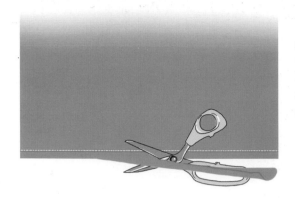

3 Cut a strip or strips from the bottom hem, if there is one. If the bottom hem is less than ½ in (1 cm) in depth, create one strip out of it by cutting above the hemming. If the bottom hem is more than ½ in (1 cm) deep, cut below the hemming so that the fabric opens up to create a normal strip. Create a separate strip from the seam left on the garment.

4 Once you have cut off all the seams, fold the garment in half lengthwise, then into quarters in the same direction, and then into eighths so that you have a tube. Remember to fold rather than roll, as thicker fabrics such as fleece become too thick to cut through when rolled. Folding lengthwise creates strips that are as long as possible.

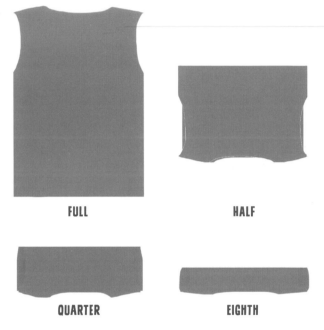

FULL   **HALF**

QUARTER   **EIGHTH**

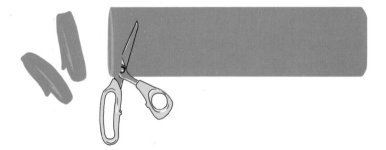

5 Cut the tube into rolls ¾ in (2 cm) wide (or whatever width the project requires). These rolls will unravel into long strips that are perfect for loopy rag rugging. Do not worry if the ends of the tube are uneven, as parts of these strips will be salvageable. Repeat this process on all the other fabric pieces. Remember to fold the sleeves lengthwise to get the longest strips possible.

USING A GAUGE

A gauge is a wonderful time- and effort-saving tool for turning longer strips into shorter ones for shaggy rag rugging. Using a gauge creates a pleasingly consistent look, as it produces fabric pieces of a similar length.

1 Cut your fabric into long strips using fabric scissors (see pages 13–14) or a rotary cutter (see page 16).

2 Hold a number of fabric strips together with the ends aligning (see box, below right). If any of the strips have a flatter end, hold that at the top. It does not matter if the strips are different lengths. Place the strips against the gauge, with the tops aligning with the groove.

3 Wind the strips around and along the gauge until you reach the ends of the strips. Shorter strips can be secured into the gauge by wrapping the longer strips over them. Overlap the edges of your strips slightly as you wind so that you cross the groove at the top of the gauge vertically. Crossing the groove diagonally creates slightly longer pieces and gives you less space on the gauge. Try not to pull the fabric too tightly as any material containing elastic will stretch, creating shorter pieces.

4 Use fabric scissors to cut along the gauge's groove. This will produce similar length, short pieces of material ideal for shaggy rag rugging. Discard any cut pieces that were too short to fit fully around the gauge.

HOW MANY STRIPS CAN I USE AT A TIME?

The number of strips wound together on the gauge depends on the thickness of the fabric and the length of the strip. Assuming a strip length of approximately 20 in (50 cm), this is the number of strips I would usually wind on the gauge at the same time. Don't worry about following this guide exactly, as thicknesses can vary.

DENIM OR FLEECE: 3 STRIPS
CLOSE-WEAVE KNIT: 4 STRIPS
T-SHIRT: 5 STRIPS
LYCRA OR COTTON: 6 STRIPS
SILK: 7 STRIPS
CHIFFON: 8 STRIPS

CUTTING STRIPS WITH A ROTARY CUTTER

Many patchworkers or crafters own a rotary cutter, cutting mat, and transparent ruler. These are great for cutting large pieces of fabric (especially bed linen) into strips quickly and neatly.

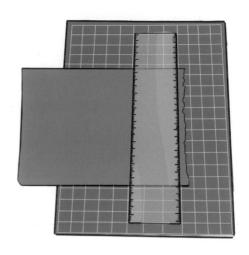

1 Remove any seams or lumps from your fabric so you have a flat piece of fabric. Fold the fabric a maximum of two times (i.e. no more than four layers in thickness) and lay it flat on the cutting mat. Align the edge of the fabric with one of the printed lines on the cutting mat as best you can. Place the ruler on top of the fabric and align it with the same printed line. Hold down the ruler firmly, making sure your fingers aren't too close to the edge of the ruler where the blade will pass by.

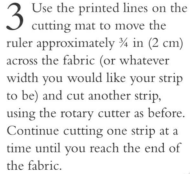

2 Starting on the cutting mat just below the edge of the fabric that is closest to you, engage the blade of the rotary cutter and cut along the edge of the ruler, moving slowly away from your body. Apply even pressure to get a clean cut and keep going until you reach the other end of the fabric. Put this end piece aside, as some but not all of it will be usable due to the fabric's ragged edge. The edge of the fabric should now be straight.

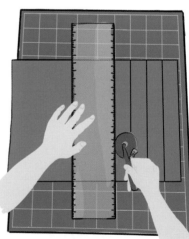

3 Use the printed lines on the cutting mat to move the ruler approximately ¾ in (2 cm) across the fabric (or whatever width you would like your strip to be) and cut another strip, using the rotary cutter as before. Continue cutting one strip at a time until you reach the end of the fabric.

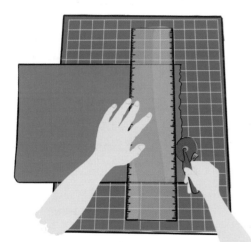

4 To turn these long strips into short strips for shaggy rag rugging, turn your cutting mat 90 degrees so that the strips are now horizontal. Repeat steps 2–3 but move the ruler at intervals of 2¾ in (7 cm).

MAKING T-SHIRT YARN

T-shirt yarn can be used to make braided rag rugs and coasters (see pages 48 and 72). Traditionally t-shirts are used, but you can add texture and create a more distressed look by using other fabrics such as cotton.

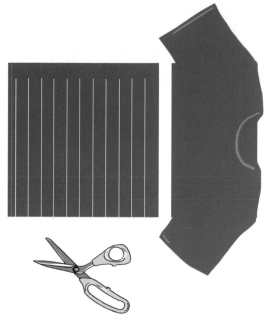

1 Lay the t-shirt flat, with one sleeve pointing toward you. Starting at the side seam closest to you and working from the hem, cut strips 2 in (5 cm) wide across the width of the t-shirt, cutting through both layers, until you are around 1¼ in (3 cm) from the far side seam. Keep going until you reach the seams of the sleeves—here you cut fully across the t-shirt to separate the neck and shoulders from the main body of the t-shirt.

2 Lay out the bottom half of the t-shirt so that the uncut side seam is on top.

3 To create a long length of fabric yarn, cut diagonally from the bottom hem of the t-shirt below the first slit and below the seam to the first slit above the seam. Continue to cut diagonally from one slit below the seam to the next slit above the seam, creating a long, continuous strand of fabric yarn. Always cut diagonally or you will create short rings of fabric as opposed to one long strip (the cutting lines are represented here by dotted lines).

4 Pull each end of the fabric strip, stretching it so that the raw edges roll in on themselves to form a "yarn."

5 Cut the remainder of the t-shirt (the shoulders and sleeves) into strips that are as long as possible, avoiding too many seams if you can. Join these strips to the long length of fabric yarn following the "Joining Strips" method (see below), and wind it all into a large ball.

JOINING STRIPS OF T-SHIRT YARN

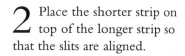

1 Align the tops of the two strips you want to join together, fold the tops over by about 1 in (2.5 cm), and cut a small slit through both layers.

2 Place the shorter strip on top of the longer strip so that the slits are aligned.

3 Pull the non-slit end of the shorter strip up through both the slits (from the bottom to the top) and pull tight to bind the strips together.

HOW TO RAG RUG

The projects in this book mainly use the loopy and shaggy rag rugging techniques, both of which can be done using a latch hook (see page 7). The third technique taught in this book—braided rag rugging—can be found in the Braided Rug on page 48.

Before starting your first project, I recommend you read "Designing for Rag Rugging" on pages 24–26, which has tips on varying these basic techniques to create different effects.

LOOPY RAG RUGGING

This is the best technique for creating defined patterns and detailed pieces. One of the great advantages of this method is that you can get into a real rhythm, and pieces grow quickly once you have mastered the technique.

1 Cut your material into long strips, approximately ¾ in (2 cm) wide (see pages 13–14). The longer the strips, the better.

2 Hold the latch hook in your main hand. Even though the latch hook has a handle, it is usually easier to hold it further down, nearer the hook, as this gives you more control.

3 Pick up a strip of fabric in your other hand. Hold the top of the strip between your index and middle fingers and further down the strip between your fourth finger and thumb. The part of the strip between your fingers should be taut. This is the part you will be hooking onto the underside of the burlap/hessian.

4 Hold the strip of fabric under the burlap. Insert the hook into your chosen hole from the top of the burlap through to the underside. The latch should be underneath the burlap and still be open.

5 Hook onto the taut part of the fabric strip. Let go of the strip with your index and middle fingers and pull the shorter end of the fabric strip up through the hole. The act of pulling the hook through the burlap forces the latch to close, trapping the fabric strip onto the hook.

> ## TIP
>
> IF YOU FIND THE LATCH IS GETTING CAUGHT IN THE BURLAP OR GENERALLY CAUSING A NUISANCE, TAPING IT OPEN HELPS. APPROXIMATELY HALF THE PEOPLE I TEACH FIND IT EASIER TO RAG RUG WITH THE LATCH TAPED OPEN.

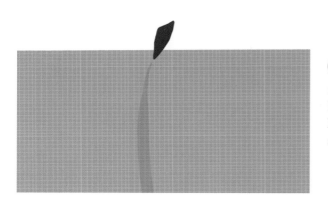

6 Adjust the end of the fabric strip so that the end sticking up is approximately ½ in (1 cm) high—or the height you would like your loops to be, as long as it is a minimum of ¼ in (5 mm) high.

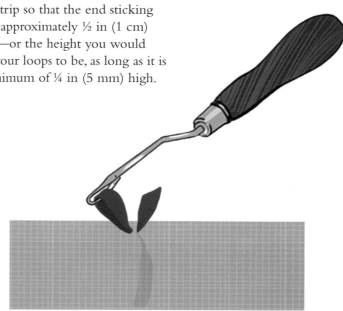

7 Working from the top of the burlap, insert the hook into the next hole in the direction you would like to rag rug (it doesn't matter if this is right, left, up, down, or diagonal). Holding the strip in whatever way you find most comfortable, hook onto the fabric strip below the burlap and pull a loop up through the burlap. The loop should be the same height as the end of the strip in the previous hole.

8 Repeat step 7 for the first four loops. The loops will begin to form a fan shape and, if you look at the underside of the burlap, you will see that the holes around the rag rugging have tightened up. This means that the rag rugging is tight enough so you no longer have to rag rug into every hole.

9 Repeat step 7 as many times as necessary, rag rugging into every other hole or two. When you reach the end of your strip or if you want to change fabric, pull the loose end of the strip through to the top of the burlap to secure. Cut it to the same height as the other loops to disguise the end.

10 If you are continuing to rag rug in the same area of the burlap, ideally you should pull the first end of the new strip up through the same hole you finished your last strip in. Having two ends in the same hole pads it out and secures everything in place, but this isn't essential. When you start a new strip in an area of burlap that already has rag rugging in it, you can continue rag rugging into every other hole or two, as the burlap has already been tightened.

COMMON MISTAKES

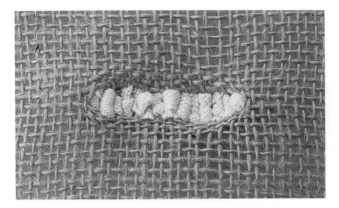

Here the rag rugging is too tight and the burlap has caved in.

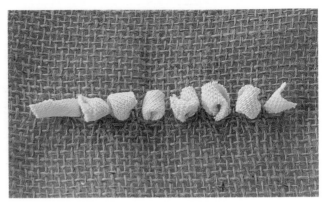

Here the rag rugging is too far apart and the burlap shows between the loops.

Missing too many holes or too few: There is no hard-and-fast rule as to the number of holes you should miss out. It depends on a number of factors including the weave of the burlap (how loose or tight), the thickness of the fabric, and the width of your strips. The maximum number of holes to miss out between one loop and the next is three, but doing this too often creates bald patches. As a general rule, if the burlap curls and puckers underneath, you are rag rugging in too many holes and if any burlap is visible from above, you are not rag rugging in enough holes. Luckily it is easy to go back and fix things.

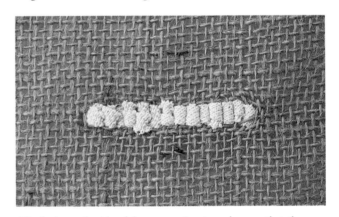

Check the underside of the rag rugging to make sure that there are no loose ends.

Not pulling ends of strips through to the top: Turn your rag rug piece over from time to time to check that there are no loose ends of strips or loops of fabric underneath. When the end of a strip has not been pulled through to the top of the burlap, it makes it vulnerable to being pulled out.

Decreasing loop size: The consistency in loop height is what makes loopy rag rugging look so neat. A common mistake made by novice rag ruggers is that they begin their loops at a certain height, then slowly decrease the loop size as they move along the strip. Although this could be a conscious design choice, rag rugging tends to look neater when it is uniform in height.

Here you can see the loops decreasing in size from left to right.

SHAGGY RAG RUGGING

Shaggy rag rugging is the more traditional technique commonly associated with historical rag rugs. It is fabulously textured and tactile—rugs made in the shaggy style are the kind you just can't wait to sink your feet into. Shaggy rag rugging tends to be more fabric-intensive than the loopy technique—on average, it uses about one third more fabric than the same area done in loopy rag rugging.

1 Cut your fabric into long strips, about ¾ in (2 cm) wide (see pages 13–14). Cut the long strips into shorter pieces approximately 2¾ in (7 cm) long, using the gauge (see page 15). You should now have a pile of short strips to practice with.

2 Hold the latch hook in your main hand. Even though the latch hook has a handle, it is usually easier to hold it further down, nearer the hook, as this gives you more control.

3 Pick up one of the short strips of fabric in your other hand. Hold the top of the strip between your index and middle fingers and the bottom of the strip between your fourth finger and thumb. The part of the strip between your fingers should be taut. This is the part you will be hooking onto on the underside of the burlap.

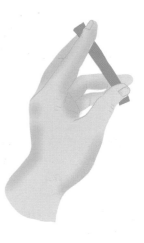

4 Hold the strip of fabric under the burlap in the location where you would like to begin. Insert the hook into your chosen hole from the top of the burlap through to the underside. The latch should be underneath the burlap and still be open at this stage. Hook onto the taut part of the fabric strip.

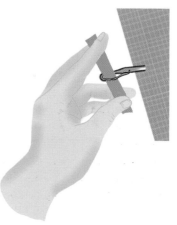

5 Let go of the top of the strip and pull one end of the strip up through the hole. It is important that you are still holding onto the other end of the fabric strip underneath the burlap or you will pull the entire strip through to the top.

6 Adjust the strip with your fingers so that about half of it is up through the burlap and half is still below.

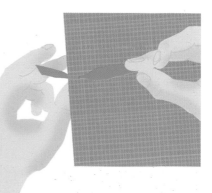

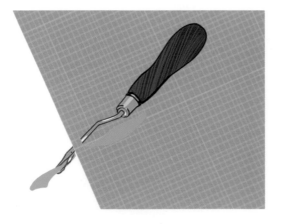

7 Insert your hook into the next hole (in whichever direction you fancy—up, down, left, right, or diagonal) from the top of the burlap to the underside again. Hook onto the strip.

8 Pull the other end of the strip up through the burlap so that the two ends are pointing upward. There should be one strand of burlap between the two ends of the strip.

9 Repeat steps 3–8 to continue this method. Your first four strips should be close together to tighten the burlap and secure everything in place. For these first strips, I recommend you rag rug the end of the new strip into a hole that already has one end of a strip in. After the first four pieces, you can miss out one to three holes between one strip and the next.

COMMON MISTAKES

Missing too many holes or too few: In shaggy rag rugging, you should never miss out too many holes between one end of the strip and the other end or you will end up with bald patches in your piece.

The maximum number of holes to miss out between one end of the strip and the other end is two, but you can miss out more holes between one strip and the next. The number of holes you can miss out depends on what the project is. Rugs get a lot of wear and tear, so you want to rag rug them tightly to ensure that they are structurally sound and well padded. Decorative items, such as wreaths, do not need to be as tightly rag rugged as they are purely esthetic. For decorative pieces, therefore, you only have to make sure that the burlap is fully covered from the front. This means that you can miss out up to five holes between strips.

As with loopy rag rugging, if the burlap begins to cave in, you are rag rugging too tightly and if any of the burlap is visible from above, you are not rag rugging closely enough (see page 20).

SHAGGY RAG RUGGING WITH THE RAG RUG SPRING TOOL

Occasionally a project requires rag rugging solely from the front of the burlap, which is when the rag rug spring tool comes into its own. With this tool, you can shaggy rag rug without access to the back of the burlap, making it perfect for joining pieces of burlap together or finishing projects after they have been assembled.

1 Cut your fabric into short pieces for shaggy rag rugging (see step 1, page 21).

2 From the top of the burlap, weave the pointed end of the rag rug spring tool down into one hole and up through a hole two or three strands away. Push enough of the tool through so that the opening of the lever is beyond the burlap strands.

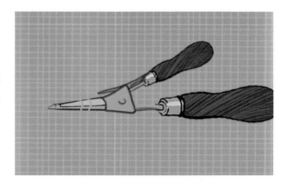

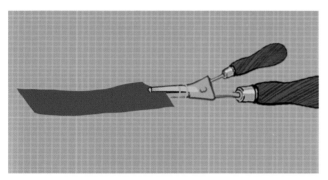

3 Squeeze the handles of the spring tool together to open up the end of the tool. Place the short end of the first fabric strip between the top and bottom parts of the tool and release the handles to clamp onto the strip.

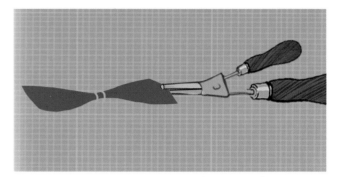

4 Pull the strip through the burlap, under the strands, so that about half of the fabric strip is on each side of the strands of burlap. This is your first rag rugged strip.

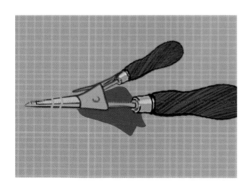

5 Repeat steps 2–4 to continue. Your first four strips should be close together to tighten the burlap and secure everything in place. For these first strips I recommend that you rag rug the end of the new strip into a hole that already has the end of a strip in it. After the first four strips, you can miss out one to three holes between one strip and the next.

TIP

IF YOU ARE USING THE RAG RUG SPRING TOOL TO JOIN TWO LAYERS OF BURLAP TOGETHER, SIMPLY FOLLOW THE INSTRUCTIONS BUT RAG RUG THROUGH THE TWO LAYERS OF BURLAP AS OPPOSED TO ONE.

DESIGNING FOR RAG RUGGING

Rag rugging is an incredibly forgiving medium. Very simple designs are often the most effective, as it is the texture that does the work for you. Here are a few tips for what to consider before embarking on any rag rug project.

THE BASICS

Some people already have a project in mind when they learn how to rag rug, but whether you have thought of a design or not, it is worth going through this checklist before starting.

Which project?

Do you need a rug? A present for a friend? A small piece to learn the techniques? Write down any specifics that are important. This could be the dimensions of the space or what you'd like to achieve out of it. You may want a rug for the hallway, for example, but it has to be flat enough for the front door to pass over.

Loopy or shaggy?

Most projects or designs lend themselves to either loopy or shaggy rag rugging, so think through which technique(s) would work best for your project.

Designs lose their definition when done in the shaggy technique, as the fabric pieces fall down in unpredictable ways. The shaggy technique generally works best either on large-scale pieces where the pattern is so big that it is unlikely to get lost or on pieces of any size with very simple designs, such as stripes, spots, checks, and geometric patterns. Shaggy rag rugging is very much about the texture, making it great for plush rugs and pillows, for example. Bear in mind that shaggy rag rugging uses more fabric than loopy, adding weight and bulk to any project.

The loopy technique is more versatile, as its compact format allows you to achieve more detailed patterns. However, even loopy rag rugging has its limitations, so I recommend choosing simple designs while you get used to the technique before moving on to advanced pieces like the Folk Art Wall Hanging (see page 80).

Combining both techniques in one project is an option, but remember that shaggy rag rugging will cover neighboring loopy rag rugging. To counter this, next to the shaggy rag rugging create a "buffer" zone of loopy rag rugging that can be partially obscured without spoiling the design. You can also vary the height of your rag rugging (see page 26) to make loopy rag rugging stand out amongst shaggy areas.

Where is your piece going?

There are few things more annoying than completing a project and realizing you're not happy with it. More often than not, this is because not enough thought has been given to where the finished piece will live and the décor surrounding it. If you are making a living-room rug, for example, which colors can you bring in from the room to tie everything together? If you are making a present for a friend, what are their favorite colors? Asking these simple questions before starting will pay off long term.

THE FINER DETAILS

Once you've decided on the most important elements of your piece, think through some of the other details.

Pattern/design

Most of us need a bit of inspiration to get the creative juices flowing. My favorite places to look are:
• Pinterest (see what I like @Raggedlife)
• Exhibitions and artists—I love Matisse, David Hockney, and Picasso for bold designs.
• Historical artifacts—especially the Celtic, Iznik, and Art Deco styles (plates and tiles are my favorites).
• Fabric patterns—I hoard Liberty of London prints!

Once you have a pattern or design in mind, ask yourself if it will work with the technique (remember, in a shaggy piece, detailed designs tend to become distorted) and is it achievable in the space available? If there is too much going on in the design, simplify it.

Color

Even more important than the design of the rag rug itself are the colors used. If you are happy with the colors and feel that they complement each other, it is difficult to go wrong. If you are unsure whether something will work, try placing colors next to each other and deciding instantly if you like them or not. Rather than selecting all your colors at the beginning of the project, add more as and when you need them. Use a blend of patterned and block colors in each project to add complexity.

As rag rugging involves upcycling old clothing and fabrics, it can be quite difficult to find the exact color you want in the quantity you need. Although this may seem irritating at the time, it is actually part of the beauty of the craft. Using similar but different shades of a color together adds intricacy and subtlety to a design. Try these techniques to help you to blend colors together.

Simple blending: Some projects (such as the Cosmic Rug on page 34) need large areas rag rugged in one color. If I were to cut up one white t-shirt, rag rug it as a block, then move on to another white t-shirt, there would be distinct blocks of unblended color, giving the rug a patchy look. Instead, I prefer to cut up multiple white t-shirts into short strips, mix all the fabrics together, and randomly rag rug with different shades of white by indiscriminately grabbing handfuls at a time. This creates a uniform background with highlights and lowlights throughout. It's a great way to disguise but make use of less appealing colors, such as gray-whites or dull blues.

Working in the round: Another way to blend colors is to make their differences part of your design. In the Teal Checkered Rug on page 32, I knew I did not have enough of one shade of teal to fill every teal square so I rag rugged around the outside of each square, then worked my way inward one row at a time using different shades of teal. This method of working inward (or outward in certain cases) and following an edge is called "working in the round."

Adding a rogue color: Finally, to really embrace the haphazard nature of rag rugging, I recommend introducing the occasional "rogue color" or patterned fabric into large blocks of color to add more intrigue and finesse to a design. This could be as subtle as a gray inserted into a blue background or as simple as a checked fabric in a block of color.

From top to bottom: t-shirt, cotton, fleece, chiffon, denim, jersey knit, Lycra (with loopy rag rugging shown on the left and shaggy rag rugging on the right).

Fabrics

Fabrics come secondary to colors in rag rugging. While it is good to have a variety of textures, I usually recommend focusing purely on colors and ignoring what the fabric is when picking out materials. This means that you will use a variety of fabrics without even thinking about it. If, however, you wish to create specific textures, the photos at the top of this page show the effects created by different fabrics when loopy and shaggy rag rugged.

T-shirt: The easiest material to rag rug with. It is perfect for beginners, as it is soft, pliable, and doesn't fray. T-shirts can be bought cheaply from charity and thrift stores and come in every color and pattern under the sun.

Cotton: One of my favorite fabrics to work with. The stiffness of the fabric tends to prop up the rag rugging and the fraying creates an interesting texture. Cotton fabrics come in a variety of lovely patterns that add depth to a project. If you prefer the cotton to fray less, cut it on the bias (at an angle to the weave of the fabric).

Fleece: One of the thickest fabrics. Cut your strips narrower (a maximum of ⅝ in/1.5 cm wide) to make rag rugging easier. Fleece has an interesting texture and bulks out the burlap/hessian.

Loop height from top to bottom: 1½ in (4 cm), 1¼ in (3 cm), ¾ in (2 cm), ⅝ in (1.5 cm), ½ in (1 cm), ¼ in (5 mm).

Fabric piece lengths from top to bottom: 3⅜ in (8.5 cm), 2¾ in (7 cm), 2¼ in (5.5 cm), 1½ in (4 cm), ¾ in (2 cm).

Chiffon: Creates a light, flouncy texture. As it is thin, cut strips wider than normal (about 1½ in/4 cm wide) and use it sparingly, as it doesn't fill the holes as well as most other fabrics. It can be slightly trickier to rag rug with, as the hook can get caught in the flimsy fabric.

Denim: By far one of the hardest materials to rag rug with, as it is thick, stiff, and frays. I recommend using other fabrics to get used to rag rugging before working your way up to denim. Use rug canvas (see page 9), as opposed to burlap, as it has a more rigid weave.

Jersey knit: I am often asked whether knitted clothing can be used in rag rugs. Yes, it can, as long as the knit has a close weave. It is great for adding texture, but tends to shed its fibers while you are working with it.

Lycra: A fun, easy fabric to use for a different texture with little effort. The high elastic content causes the fabric to curl into tubes that look very impressive mixed in with other materials.

4. Varied height
A great way to add depth and complexity to any design is to vary the height of your loopy or shaggy rag rugging. This can be an easy way to make certain elements in your piece stand out.

Loopy rag rugging: Most people have a natural height at which they rag rug loops—this tends to be around ½–¾ in (1–2 cm). Loopy rag rugging is flexible, as very short loops can be used to create detailed, compact patterns or, at the other end of the scale, large loops can be used for a petal effect. The swatch above left shows how loop heights can be used to different effect. The "Spring is in the Air" basket on page 102 shows how short and long loops are used in the same project.

Shaggy rag rugging: The height of shaggy rag rugging is determined by the length of the fabric strips used. If using a gauge, your strips will be uniform in length (around 2¾ in/7 cm, which is perfect for rugs). To create a different pile you can cut your fabric pieces longer or shorter. The photo above shows how different fabric lengths look when shaggy rag rugged.

TIP

USE FABRICS WITH SENTIMENTAL VALUE TO WEAVE MEMORIES INTO YOUR RAG RUGGING. THIS COULD BE CHILDREN'S OLD CLOTHING, CURTAINS FROM YOUR FIRST HOME, OR A SARONG BOUGHT ON A MEMORABLE VACATION… ANYTHING GOES.

CARING FOR YOUR RAG RUG

Over time, rugs get a lot of wear and tear—people tramping back and forth, things being spilled, and dust simply gathering. With a wool rug, cleaning is simply a case of regular vacuuming and putting in a bit of elbow grease with a carpet cleaner as and when it's needed. Rag rugs are completely different: they should never be vacuumed, as the pieces of fabric may be pulled out. Here's how to keep your rag rugs clean or wash them when they get dirty.

Never back your rag rugs
Dust and grime get trapped between the rag rugging and backing and once it's in, it is impossible to get out. In particular, grit caught in rugs can wear them out from the inside.

Regularly shake the rug outside
Shaking the rug forces out all the dust and debris that have collected between the fabric strips. Shaking has the added benefit of plumping up a rug that has become flattened over time. I sometimes hang my rugs over the washing line and beat them to give them a more thorough airing.

Machine-washing a rag rug
• Place the rag rug in a pillowcase, then put it into the drum of the washing machine. If possible, tie the pillowcase closed so that the rug does not fall out during the washing process.

• Wash the rug on the coolest and gentlest setting of your washing machine using a mild detergent.

• Once the cycle has finished, take the rug out of the washing machine. Don't worry if a few pieces have fallen out. You can either hook these back into your rug when it is dry or discard them as they may not be noticed. They are but a drop in the ocean!

• Hang the rug outside on a washing line or on a clothes horse. At the end of the day, if it is still not dry, put it inside the house where you would normally do your drying.

Before you do this, a few words of warning:

• Never wash a partially made rag rug. In the washing process, any burlap/hessian that isn't rag rugged will shrink to a much tighter weave.

• Choose a sunny day because rag rugs should be air dried outside where possible. Never dry a rag rug in the tumble dryer.

• Think carefully before washing vintage rag rugs in the washing machine. The burlap will have weakened over time, making the rug more vulnerable to falling apart. Where possible, wash vintage rugs by hand.

Sponge the rag rug with fabric cleaner as soon as any spillage occurs
Rag rugs are simply made from old fabric so, if applied soon enough, a good fabric cleaner should remove most stains.

Re-rag part of the rug
I only recommend this method if nothing else can be done, e.g. red wine stains that cannot be removed. Replacing the rags in a certain area is the best way to ensure that the rug looks as good as new.

Chapter 1   **RUGS**

SCANDI STRIPED RUG

This super-chic Scandinavian-inspired rug is the perfect project for those looking to create a modern rug that will look great in any room in the house. Neutral colored fabrics are some of the easiest to track down (I've used solid colors and patterns), and a little bit of sparkle looks great in this rug. The striped pattern is a simple but effective design whether you are looking to make your first rug or are a veteran of the craft.

YOU WILL NEED

Burlap/hessian

Tape measure

Marker pen

Everyday scissors

Sewing machine or needle and thread

Assorted fabrics

Fabric scissors

Gauge

Latch hook

COLOR PALETTE

Black, gray, cream, navy, white

1 Use a tape measure and marker pen to draw a 57 x 26-in (145 x 65-cm) rectangle on the burlap/hessian. Try to keep in line with the weave of the burlap as much as possible (see page 10). Edge hem all around the rug (see pages 11–12) using a needle and thread or a sewing machine. This will reduce the size of the rug slightly.

2 Choose the fabric you would like to use for the first row of your rug and cut it into short strips for shaggy rag rugging using fabric scissors and the gauge (see pages 13–15). You will usually get one or two rows out of a medium-sized garment—it takes more fabric than you would think!

3 Shaggy rag rug (see pages 21–22) one row along the short edge of the rug, keeping close to the edge. You do not need to rag rug through the hem of the rug, as the shaggy fabric pieces will disguise the edging.

4 Once you have reached the end of your first row, miss out one row of holes in the burlap, change fabric color, and rag rug your second row next to your first. I find it helps to rag rug all your rows in the same direction so that you can get into a rhythm.

5 Once you reach the end of your second row, repeat step 4 but miss out two or three rows of holes between each row of shaggy rag rugging. Continue until you reach the other end of the rug.

TIP

I RECOMMEND RAG RUGGING THE OUTSIDE OF THE BLOCKS FIRST AND WORKING YOUR WAY IN TO GIVE THE RUG A MORE SYMMETRICAL APPEARANCE. IF YOU WOULD LIKE A MORE RANDOM LOOK, YOU CAN FILL IN THE BLOCKS ONE AT A TIME.

TEAL CHECKERED RUG

When people begin rag rugging, it's usually with the ambition of making a rug—this is the original purpose of the craft, after all. If you'd like to make a rug as your first project, this bathroom mat is a great place to start. Bathroom rugs don't have to be particularly large and won't be on display to the world if anything happens to go awry, plus they're practical because they keep your feet off the cold floor and mop up any water overflow.

1 Use a tape measure and marker pen to draw a 39 x 24-in (100 x 60-cm) rectangle on the burlap/hessian. Try to keep in line with the weave of the burlap as much as possible (see page 10). Edge hem all around the rug (see pages 11–12) using a needle and thread or a sewing machine. This will reduce the size of the rug slightly.

2 Measure and draw lines on the burlap to divide the rug into nine blocks lengthwise and five blocks widthwise. Use the marker pen to write "T" or "W" in each block to show which will be teal and which will be white (I like having teal in the four corners of the rug). Don't worry if the blocks are not completely square as this is part of the design.

3 Prepare your teal fabrics for loopy rag rugging by cutting them into long strips (see pages 13–14), approximately ¾ in (2 cm) in width.

4 Loopy rag rug (see pages 18–19) your first row around the outside of one of the "T" corner blocks. Your loops should be approximately ⅝–¾ in (1.5–2 cm) in height. Rag rug through any hemming to ensure that none of the burlap is visible.

5 Using the same fabric, loopy rag rug around the edge of each of the "T" blocks across the rug. Assess how much of the first fabric you have left. If you have enough to do another row inside each "T" block, then rag rug a second row. If not, change to a different shade of teal and rag rug along the inside of each "T" block, keeping close to the first row of rag rugging. Keep going, changing to a new shade of teal as and when you need it, until all the teal squares are full (see working in the round, page 25).

6 Prepare your white fabrics for loopy rag rugging. Fill in the "W" blocks—as with the teal, loopy rag rug in concentric squares to blend the different shades of white together (you'd be surprised how many different shades there are!). Keep going until the whole rug is rag rugged and no burlap is visible.

YOU WILL NEED

Burlap/hessian

Tape measure

Marker pen

Everyday scissors

Sewing machine or needle and thread

Ruler

Assorted fabrics

Fabric scissors

Latch hook

COLOR PALETTE

Teals, whites

COSMIC RUG

For this square rug I hoarded white t-shirts for a while, then sourced the bright colors from thrift/charity stores and friends. The thrill of the chase then comes in, as you try to track down a sizzling orange, vibrant green, or hot pink. I think using patterned and plain fabrics together works particularly well here, as the large circles need variety to break them up. It's like looking at the planets, which is why I've called it my "Cosmic Rug."

YOU WILL NEED

Burlap/hessian

Tape measure

Marker pen

Everyday scissors

Sewing machine or needle and thread

Plates of different diameters (optional)

Assorted fabrics

Fabric scissors

Gauge

Latch hook

COLOR PALETTE

Pinks, oranges, greens, bright and pale yellows, whites

1 Use a tape measure and marker pen to draw a 43 x 43-in (110 x 110-cm) square on the burlap/hessian. Try to keep in line with the weave of the burlap as much as possible (see page 10). Edge hem all around the rug (see pages 11–12) using a needle and thread or a sewing machine. This will reduce the size of the rug slightly.

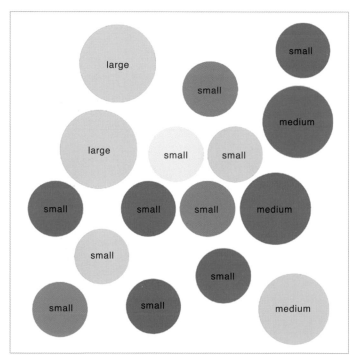

Color guide

2 Draw 16 circles of varying sizes on the burlap. I randomly drew around plates of three different sizes to create my design, but you can copy the color guide above if you wish. Choose the color for each circle and color code the burlap by writing the colors inside the circles. I have four pink circles, three orange circles, three green circles, five bright yellow circles, and one pale yellow circle.

3 Choose the color palette for your first circle and cut your material into short strips for shaggy rag rugging using the gauge (see pages 13–15). Mix the fabrics together and shaggy rag rug (see pages 21–22) the circle, making sure that the different shades are blended well. Repeat until all the circles are rag rugged.

4 Cut the white fabric for the background into short pieces for shaggy rag rugging (see pages 13–15). Fill in the background by shaggy rag rugging, taking care to mix various shades of white together as you go to avoid ending up with blocks of unblended color (see simple blending, page 25).

"SPLASH OF SUMMER" RUG

This rug is as much a piece of art as it is a rug—I sometimes display it as a wall hanging when I need a change of scenery. This is a fairly advanced project that gives you the opportunity to get creative. The wonky petals of the flower make for a slightly whimsical and playful look that can only really be achieved by letting the rug grow organically and sketching things out by hand. Try not to worry too much about right and wrong while rag rugging this piece—just add colors in as and when you feel like it. This way you'll create a truly unique rug to your personal taste.

1 Use a tape measure and marker pen to draw a 35½ x 35½-in (90 x 90-cm) square on the burlap/hessian. Try to keep in line with the weave of the burlap as much as possible (see page 10). Edge hem all around the rug (see pages 11–12) using a needle and thread or a sewing machine. This will reduce the size of the rug slightly.

2 Using a tape measure, measure diagonally from one corner to the opposite one and draw a small mark where the lines cross—this is the center of the rug. Copy the circle template on page 122 and draw around it in the center of the burlap—this will be center of your flower.

3 Draw a 31½-in (80-cm) diameter circle centrally on the burlap. The best way to do this is to tie a marker pen to a piece of string that is 15¾ in (40 cm) long plus the extra string required for attaching the pen. Pin the end of the string without the pen to the center of the burlap (or ask a friend to hold it in place) and stretch the string out taut. With the pen in a vertical position, move slowly in a clockwise direction, marking out the circle.

TIP

IT IS VERY IMPORTANT THAT THE BURLAP DOESN'T SHIFT DURING THIS STAGE. TAPING IT TO THE FLOOR CAN HELP TO KEEP IT IN PLACE.

YOU WILL NEED

Burlap/hessian

Tape measure

Marker pen

Everyday scissors

Sewing machine or needle and thread

Ruler

String

Thumbtack/drawing pin (optional)

Sticky tape (optional)

Templates on page 122 (optional)

Assorted fabrics

Fabric scissors

Latch hook

COLOR PALETTE

Pinks, pale yellow, red, light blue, light purple, dark patterned

4 Draw eight petals around the center of the flower. I drew the petals by hand so they were all different shapes and sizes for a slightly quirky look, but if you wish you can use the templates on page 122. Sketch out eight evenly spaced circles around the large circle, either freehand or using the large template on page 122. Measure in 13¾ in (35 cm) from each corner of the burlap and make a mark on the edge of the burlap. Draw a diagonal line to join the marks in each corner together. Draw a circle in each of the four corner triangles either freehand or using the large template on page 122.

5 Cut the pink and pale yellow fabrics into long strips ¾ in (2 cm) wide for loopy rag rugging (see pages 13–14). Loopy rag rug (see pages 18–19) the center of the flower and the edge of each of the petals in pink fabric (see the color guide below). Your loops should be about ⅝–¾ in (1.5–2 cm) in height. Use the yellow fabric strips to loopy rag rug the inside of each of the petals.

6 Loopy rag rug two rows around the large central circle in a dark patterned fabric—this adds contrast to the rug. Loopy rag rug the eight circles around the edge of the dark circle by mixing shades of pink, red, yellow, and patterned fabric. Fill in the rest of the large central circle in different shades of light blue and purple. Mix in patterned fabrics now and then.

7 Loopy rag rug the border and corner bars of the rug in light blue. The edge of the rug should have three rows of light blue rag rugging and the corner bars should be two rows wide. Mix the light blues thoroughly before beginning to rag rug to add variety to the rug.

8 Fill in the area between the circle and corner bars in a mixture of light purples. Rag rug the circles in each corner of the rug in a mixture of bright fabrics, then fill in the rest of the burlap with light blue or purple rag rugging.

Color guide

DENIM CHEVRON RUG

One of the most classic fashion pairings is a simple white shirt with jeans. It's versatile yet timeless, and formed the inspiration for this rug. Using nine pairs of jeans and eight white shirts donated to me by a local company (fortunately for me they'd had a uniform change), this rug was a real labor of love. Denim is a great material because it is so hard-wearing, but it can be challenging to work with as it is tough to cut up and rough on the hands. This is a project for more experienced rag ruggers.

1 Measure and mark out a 37 x 27½-in (94 x 70-cm) rectangle on the rug canvas. Rug canvas needs securing if the edges are not selvages, so I hemmed two edges of this rug using the seams of jeans. Find three pairs of jeans that are a similar color (here a medium shade of blue). Turn the jeans inside out and cut the seams off the outside legs, 1¼ in (3 cm) away from the seam itself. Cut any bulk off the top or bottom of the strip.

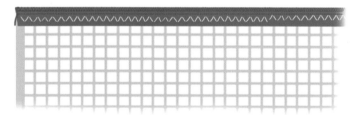

2 Sandwich the canvas edge inside the seam and pin it in place. Cut to length if necessary. Machine stitch along the seam using a zig zag stitch, securing the canvas inside. Repeat so that all the loose edges of the canvas are hemmed. You may need two seams for each long edge of the rug. If so, overlap the ends of the two seams when sewing them to the canvas.

3 Cut the rest of the three pairs of medium blue jeans into long strips for loopy rag rugging (see pages 13–14). The strips should be as long as possible but only about ½ in (1 cm) in width to compensate for the thickness of the denim. (Do not use any seams for rag rugging, as these are too thick when using denim.)

YOU WILL NEED

37 x 27½ in (94 x 70 cm) 3HPI (holes per inch) mesh rug canvas (ideally two sides should be selvages)

Tape measure

Marker pen

Everyday scissors

Fabrics—denim and white shirts

Fabric scissors

Pins

Sewing machine and denim-colored thread

Latch hook

COLOR PALETTE

Blue (I used six different shades), white

4 Loopy rag rug one row (see pages 18–19) along one
short edge of the canvas, close to the hem. Your loops
should be about ¾ in (2 cm) in height so that the denim
stays secure. Rag rug three more rows of denim, working
toward the center of the rug (making a total of four rows),
to form a block of denim at the end of the rug. Repeat
these four rows at the other short edge of the canvas.

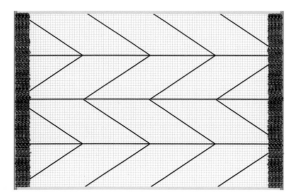

5 Measure and divide the remaining bare canvas into
four widthwise and lengthwise. Draw three long lines
along the length of the canvas. To create the chevrons, draw
diagonal lines as shown above.

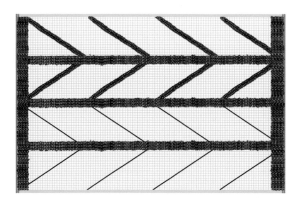

6 Using the same shade of denim as the blocks at
the ends of the rug, loopy rag rug three rows along
each of the three long lines of the rug. In the same
shade of denim, loopy rag rug two rows along each
of the diagonal chevron lines.

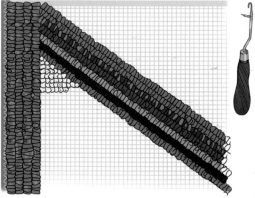

7 Loopy rag rug five diagonal rows in different shades of
denim, as above. Cut the white shirts into long strips
for loopy rag rugging (see pages 13–14). Shirt fabric is
much thinner than denim, so add thickness by using two
strips at once—hold two similar-length strips together with
the ends aligned and loopy rag rug as if the two strips were
one. When you reach the end of one or both strips, pull
them through to the top and cut both strips to ¾ in (2 cm)
in height (the same height as the denim loops). Loopy rag
rug the rest of the canvas with shirts in this way.

RAINBOW RUG

This rag rug is one of my absolute all-time favorites, not just because of the design but because of what it is made from and what it represents. It is the original "memory mat" made from clothing that my brother and I had as children. I look at this rug and can recognize a bright orange swimsuit from when I was nine years old, a Cancun t-shirt bought on a family vacation to Mexico, and school uniforms from across the ages. Rag rugging is a great way to weave memories into your home and it sure beats having precious clothing stored in dusty boxes in the attic.

YOU WILL NEED

Burlap/hessian

Tape measure

Marker pen

Everyday scissors

Sewing machine or needle and thread

Assorted fabrics

Fabric scissors

Gauge

Latch hook

COLOR PALETTE

All the colors of the rainbow and more!

1 Use a tape measure and marker pen to draw a 51 x 35½-in (130 x 90-cm) rectangle on the burlap/hessian. Try to keep in line with the weave of the burlap as much as possible (see page 10). Edge hem all around the rug (see pages 11–12) using a needle and thread or a sewing machine. This will reduce the size of the rug slightly.

2 Choose the fabric you would like to use for the first row of your rug (I've used green at each end of the rug). Cut your material into short strips for shaggy rag rugging using fabric scissors and the gauge (see pages 13–15).

3 Shaggy rag rug (see pages 21–22) one row along the short edge of the rug, keeping close to the edge of the burlap. You do not need to rag rug through the hem of the rug, as the shaggy fabric pieces will disguise the edging.

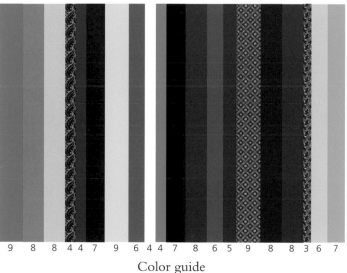

4 Continue rag rugging one row at a time until you reach the other end of the rug. I recommend leaving two or three rows of empty holes between each row of rag rugging. I have rag rugged in color blocks roughly following the color guide on the left (the number of rows are at the bottom of the guide), but feel free to rag rug in whatever order you fancy. Interspersing random rows of patterned fabrics works well in this rug.

IZNIK RUG

One question I am often asked is where my design ideas come from. As with most designers, inspiration comes from a number of places, but one source I come back to time and time again is historical artifacts. I love spending time at London's British Museum or Victoria & Albert Museum and studying the Celtic bracelets, antique Chinese furniture, or Renaissance silverware. This particular rug was inspired by an Iznik plate.

YOU WILL NEED

Burlap/hessian

Tape measure

String

Thumbtack/drawing pin (optional)

Marker pen

Sticky tape (optional)

Sewing machine and thread

Everyday scissors

Ruler

Pins

Templates on page 122

Assorted fabrics

Fabric scissors

Gauge

Latch hook

COLOR PALETTE

Red, green, navy, white, black

1 Draw a 39-in (1-m) diameter circle on the burlap/hessian. See step 3 on page 37 for the method, but for this project the string needs to be 19½ in (50 cm) long.

TIP

IT IS VERY IMPORTANT THAT THE BURLAP DOESN'T SHIFT DURING THIS STAGE, SO TAPING IT TO THE FLOOR CAN HELP TO KEEP IT IN PLACE.

2 Hem around the circumference of the circle using placeholder hemming stitch (see page 13). Cut off any loose threads. Cut the circle out, keeping as close to the stitching as possible without cutting the stitches. The edge of your circle may curl slightly, but this is normal.

3 The circle now needs to be edge hemmed (see pages 11–12). The edge of the burlap needs to be turned over by ½ in (1 cm), but to stop it from curling, you will need to create small pleats in the hem as you fold it. You will not be rag rugging through the hemming so the thickness is not an issue. Try to space these pleats out evenly around the circle. Pin the pleats as you go, then machine stitch the hem in place using a simple straight stitch.

4 Now draw the pattern on the burlap using a marker pen. First sketch a circle 4 in (10 cm) from the outside of the rug using the string-and-pen method described in step 1. Then use the templates on page 122 and the color guides at right to build up the rest of the design.

5 Cut your fabrics into short strips for shaggy rag rugging (see pages 13–15). First shaggy rag rug (see pages 21–22) the inside circle of the rug (if you rag rug the border of the rug first it weighs down the outside, making rag rugging near the center harder). I recommend rag rugging the red sections first, then the green, then the navy, and finally the white.

6 When the center is complete, shaggy rag rug the border, starting with the red sections, then their surrounding white blocks, and finally fill in the rest of the rug with a mixture of navy, black, and white.

Color guide for the center

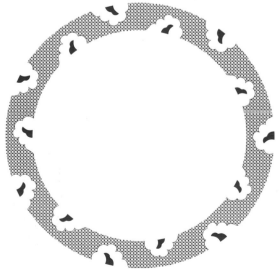

Color guide for the border

TIP

IF YOU ARE UP FOR A CHALLENGE, TRY TO MAKE THE STRIPES INCREASE IN WIDTH THE FURTHER OUT THEY STRETCH. DO THIS BY GRADUALLY INCREASING THE NUMBER OF HOLES BETWEEN THE THREE ROWS AS YOU RAG RUG. FILL IN WITH RANDOM PIECES OF WHITE FABRIC IF ANY OF THE BURLAP IS SHOWING.

AMMONITE RUG

I have always loved the striped shape of ammonite fossils, and this inspired the design of this rug. However, rather than staying true to the ammonite's neutral, earthy colors, I decided to add a twist. My father did some charity work in Uganda and, knowing my love of fabric, brought some gorgeous print fabric home for me. This rug is made almost entirely of that fabric, rag rugged in stripes between the white structure of the ammonite.

1 Use a tape measure and marker pen to draw a 54 x 39-in (130 x 100-cm) rectangle on the burlap/hessian. Try to keep in line with the weave of the burlap as much as possible (see page 10). Edge hem all around the rug (see pages 11–12) using a needle and thread or a sewing machine. This will reduce the size of the rug slightly. Enlarge the ammonite template on page 122 and draw it onto the burlap.

2 Cut the fabrics into short strips for shaggy rag rugging using the gauge (see pages 13–15). Shaggy rag rug (see pages 21–22) around the central circle of the ammonite in white, then shaggy rag rug two rows in white along the curve of the ammonite.

YOU WILL NEED

Burlap/hessian

Tape measure

Marker pen

Everyday scissors

Sewing machine or needle and thread

Assorted fabrics

Fabric scissors

Gauge

Latch hook

COLOR PALETTE

White, multicolors, lilac

Color guide

3 Still using the white fabric, rag rug three rows for each of the stripes of the ammonite (also see tip on the far left).

4 Fill in each of the sections of the ammonite in stripes of multicolored fabric, working from the inside of the ammonite outward. If you would like your rug to take on a hint of one particular color, intersperse the multicolored fabrics with a stripe of block color—here I've used lilac.

BRAIDED RUG

Braided rag rugs have been appearing all over social media recently as a fun way to upcycle old t-shirts into something both beautiful and useful. One of the greatest draws is that you don't need much specialist equipment. In fact, you probably have everything you need at home already! As long as you choose colors you love, then it is very difficult to go wrong with the design and the only slightly tricky part is stitching the braid together. My advice is to take your time to make sure that the rug lies perfectly flat in the end.

YOU WILL NEED

Assorted fabrics (I used 14 t-shirts to make a rug 45 x 33½ in/115 x 85 cm)

Fabric scissors

Bag clip or clothespin/peg

Ruler or tape measure

Pins

Needle and thread (I used button or extra-strong thread)

COLOR PALETTE

Assorted colors—see tip

1 Choose 14 plain t-shirts in various colors for your rug. Turn all the t-shirts into balls of fabric yarn (see page 17).

2 Choose the three colors you would like at the center of your rug. I recommend choosing at least one "neutral" color to start with (see tip below). Tie the ends of the three yarns together to form a knot. Weigh down the knot with something heavy to make the braiding easier.

TIP

I LIKE TO USE AT LEAST FOUR "NEUTRAL" COLORS (HERE I'VE USED TWO WHITES, LIGHT AND DARK GRAY, AND NAVY) TO GROUND THE COLOR SCHEME. I MAINLY USE SOLID COLORS (AS OPPOSED TO PATTERNED T-SHIRTS) TO CREATE A BOLD PALETTE. BEFORE TURNING YOUR T-SHIRTS INTO FABRIC YARN, PLACE THEM NEXT TO EACH OTHER TO MAKE SURE THE COLORS COMPLEMENT EACH OTHER. IF ANY OF THE FABRICS LOOK OUT OF PLACE, CHOOSE A DIFFERENT COLOR TO REPLACE THEM.

3 Braid/plait the three yarns together, making sure to keep the braid fairly loose. Secure the braid as you go using a clip or clothespin/peg. As you braid, try to tuck in any seams so that they are on the underside of the braid—the tidier you can keep the top of the braid, the neater your rug will look. During braiding the fabric strands will get tangled in a counter-braid further down the yarn, so untangle them from time to time. Wind the braid into a ball as you go.

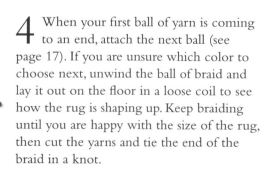

TIP

BEFORE BRAIDING, THINK THROUGH HOW YOU WOULD LIKE YOUR RUG TO LOOK. BRAIDING SIMILAR SHADES TOGETHER CREATES A BOLD COLOR BAND IN THE RUG, WHILE MIXING DIFFERENT COLORS TOGETHER CREATES A "SPECKLED" LOOK. DO NOT OVERANALYZE YOUR DESIGN—IF YOU ARE HAPPY WITH THE COLORS YOU'VE CHOSEN, THEN IT IS HARD TO GO WRONG. THE COLORS NATURALLY BLEND TOGETHER AS ONE BRAIDED COLOR ENDS AND THE NEXT YARN IS ADDED IN.

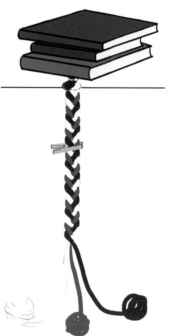

4 When your first ball of yarn is coming to an end, attach the next ball (see page 17). If you are unsure which color to choose next, unwind the ball of braid and lay it out on the floor in a loose coil to see how the rug is shaping up. Keep braiding until you are happy with the size of the rug, then cut the yarns and tie the end of the braid in a knot.

5 Carefully wind the braid into a large ball. The end of the braid that you would like on the outside of your rug should be at the center of the ball.

BEFORE YOU START ASSEMBLING THE RUG

The hardest part of this project is achieving a rag rug that lies perfectly flat. When sewing your braid together, make sure you leave enough excess braid around any curves in the rug. This will prevent your rug from curling up like a bowl.

6 Place the beginning of the braid upside down (you will be sewing on the slightly messier side) and measure 22 in (56 cm) from the end of the braid. Bend the braid back on itself (all the time keeping the braid facing downward) and pin the bend in the braid together to make sewing easier.

7 Starting at the bend in the braid, sew the two inner edges of the braid together tightly so that the stitches are not visible from the neat side of the braid (fortunately it doesn't matter what it looks like from the back!). When you reach the knotted end of the braid, cut off the knot and sew the loose edge on top of the bend in the braid (still on the underside) to secure it in place.

8 Continue sewing the braid together in a clockwise direction. It is extremely important that you feed the braid loosely around the corners (so that there is excess braid around any curves) or the rug will curl up. It helps to lay your rug on the floor every now and then to make sure that it is lying flat.

TIP

IF YOU FIND THAT YOUR FINISHED RUG DOES NOT LIE FLAT, STRETCHING THE RUG OUT AND ATTACHING NON-SLIP BACKING MAY FIX THE PROBLEM. OTHERWISE, LIGHTLY DAMPENING THE RUG, THEN STEAMING IT FLAT WITH AN IRON CAN HELP.

9 Continue sewing your braid in a clockwise direction until you are happy with the size of the rug. It is best to attach the end of your braid to the curved corner of the rug rather than a long, straight edge so that it blends in. Trim the end of the braid and overlap it with the braid inside. Sew it on top to secure the rug.

GARDEN GREEN RUG

One of the easiest and most effective patterns you can use in rag rug is a simple striped design. It means that you can rag rug following the weave of the burlap and break up the rug into manageable chunks, taking it one row at a time. Although I love rag rugging in stripes, it can get a little monotonous. To mix things up a bit, this rug has stripes in both directions, which breaks up the pattern and makes things more visually interesting.

1 Use a tape measure and marker pen to draw a 40 x 60-in (102 x 152-cm) rectangle on the burlap/hessian. Try to keep in line with the weave of the burlap as much as possible (see page 10). Edge hem all around the rug (see pages 11–12) using a needle and thread or a sewing machine. This will reduce the size of the rug slightly.

2 Cut your first fabric into long strips for loopy rag rugging (see pages 13–14). I've used a charcoal color to start with.

3 Loopy rag rug (see pages 18–19) in a row along the short edge of the rug, keeping as close to the edge as possible. If the edge is hemmed, rather than a selvage, rag rug through the hemming. This can be a bit tough but it is necessary to make sure no that burlap is visible. It also makes the edge doubly secure.

4 Continue loopy rag rugging 33 more rows following the sequence shown in color guide 1 (below—the numbers indicate the amount of rows). Each rag rug is entirely unique so if you don't have a particular color available, feel free to substitute it with another. Just make sure that your color complements the overall palette of the rug—any shade of green should be a safe bet!

1 3   3 1   5   1 3   2   3 1 1 3   5   1 1

Color guide 1

YOU WILL NEED

Burlap/hessian

Tape measure

Ruler

Marker pen

Everyday scissors

Sewing machine or needle and thread

Assorted fabrics

Fabric scissors

Latch hook

COLOR PALETTE

Greens, grays, tan, charcoal, light yellow

5 Once you have finished the first 34 rows, measure out and mark a line on the burlap 17¾ in (45 cm) from the rows you have just rag rugged. This line runs across the burlap from one long edge to the opposite side.

6 Change direction and loopy rag rug up to the drawn line using the sequence shown in color guide 2 (right). This should be approximately 137 rows, but don't worry if yours is slightly different. Here your rows run parallel to the long edges.

7 Once this section is complete, change direction again and rag rug 38 rows using the sequence shown in color guide 3 (below). Here your rows run parallel to the short edges.

8 After finishing the third section, change direction again and finish off by rag rugging 124 rows in the sequence shown in color guide 4 (right). Your rows should reach right up to the edge of the rug, rag rugging through the hem if necessary (as you did in the very first row).

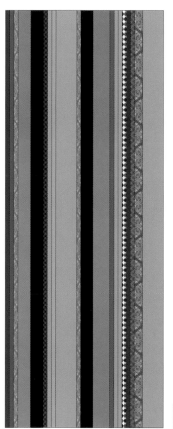

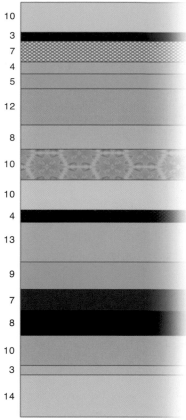

10
3
7
4
5
12
8
10
10
4
13
9
7
8
10
3
14

Color guide 2

Color guide 4

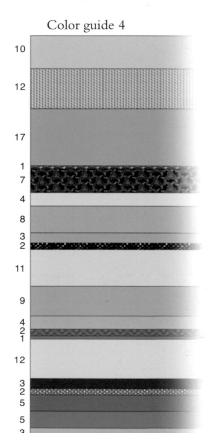

10
12
17
1
7
4
8
3
2
11
9
4
2
1
12
3
2
5
5
3
3

1 1 1   3   3 1 1 1   5   1   3   4   1 1 1 1 1 1 2   5

Color guide 3

Chapter 2 **HOME ACCESSORIES AND GIFTS**

RAGGED LIFE LETTERS

Rag rug letters make fabulous personalized gifts for anyone, whatever their age. You can rag rug a friend's initial in the colors they like, or even go one step further and use fabrics that have sentimental value (such as clothes that children have outgrown).

1 Copy your letter from the templates on pages 124–125, enlarging it to the correct size. Place the letter template on the foamboard and draw around it using a marker pen.

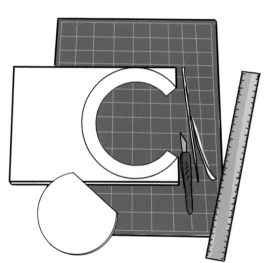

2 Use a metal ruler and scalpel to cut along any straight parts of the letter (do not use a plastic ruler as the blade of the scalpel may slip). Protect your work surface by using a cutting mat. Cut out the rest of the letter carefully with the scalpel. Don't worry if your lines are slightly crooked, as this is just the base for your letter and won't be visible.

3 Place your foamboard template face up on the burlap/hessian, leaving at least 3½ in (9 cm) of cloth between the letter and the edge of the burlap. Draw around the letter using a marker pen. Set the foamboard aside.

TIP

IF YOU DO NOT HAVE FOAMBOARD, THICK CARDBOARD CAN BE USED AS AN ALTERNATIVE BUT IT MUST BE AT LEAST ¼ IN (5 MM) THICK OR THE LETTER WILL NOT BE VERY STURDY.

YOU WILL NEED

¼-in (5-mm) thick foamboard (or cardboard—see tip)

Marker pen

Metal ruler

Scalpel (with sharp blade)

Cutting mat

Burlap/hessian

Sewing machine and thread

Everyday scissors

Fabric scissors

Assorted fabrics in black and your choice of colors

Latch hook

Staple gun

Felt (optional)

Glue gun (optional)

D-ring picture hook (optional)

COLOR PALETTE

Black border, any color inner

4 Use the sewing machine to hem around the outline of the letter using one row of placeholder hemming stitch (see page 13). This will hold the rag rugging in place.

5 Draw and then machine stitch another hem around the drawn letter, using placeholder hemming stitch again. This should be a continuous hem approximately 1¼ in (3 cm) outside the original letter. If the letter has an enclosed center (like A, B, D, etc), you will need to create a hem within the enclosed part(s) of the letters, too. This hemming is to prevent the burlap fraying and falling apart when you cut out the letter later. Cut off any loose threads.

6 Choose the fabric for your border—I recommend black, as it makes the letter stand out. Cut this fabric into long strips for loopy rag rugging (see pages 13–14).

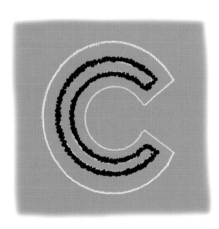

7 In black, loopy rag rug (see pages 18–19) around the outline of the letter, just on the outside of the first hem you stitched (this row of rag rugging will cover the sides of the letter). Make sure you rag rug on the side of the burlap that you drew your letter on, or your letter will be back to front.

8 Fill in the letter in loopy rag rugging in whatever colors and pattern you fancy. I find that stripes are very effective.

9 Once the letter is fully rag rugged, cut away the excess burlap by trimming along the edge of the outside hem of the letter, keeping as close to the stitches as possible. Be careful not to cut any of the stitches. If the letter has an enclosed center (like A, B, D, etc), cut out the inside.

10 Place the rag rugged letter with the loops face down. Place your foamboard letter on top, aligning the edges of the rag rugging with the edges of the letter. Fold the outer hem of the burlap around the edge of the letter and secure it to the foamboard using a staple gun.

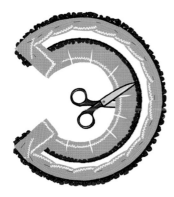

11 If the letter has an enclosed center or curves inward, you will need to make small cuts in the burlap in certain areas to secure the letter to the foamboard. Do not worry if the burlap frays a little—it will still hold everything in place.

12 If you want to tidy up the back of the letter, cut a piece of felt to the correct letter shape and glue it to the back. Attach a D-ring picture hook so that the letter can be hung—work out where the center of gravity of your letter is before attaching the D-ring, to ensure that it will hang straight.

CHALKBOARD FRAME

If you like to write lists or inspiring words of wisdom, a chalkboard is fun to display on a shelf or hang in the bedroom or kitchen. The fabric frame can be multi-colored, as shown here, or made in varying shades to tone with the décor of your room. This project is great for using up small pieces of leftover fabric, and it's a good way of practicing your rag rugging skills for larger projects later on!

YOU WILL NEED

Wooden photo frame

Burlap/hessian

Marker pen

Ruler

Sewing machine and thread

Assorted fabrics

Fabric scissors

Gauge

Latch hook

Everyday scissors

Staple gun

Newspaper

Paint brush

Chalkboard paint

COLOR PALETTE

Any colors—use a good mixture of different colors across the whole frame

1 Take the backing board and any glass out of the photo frame. Place the empty frame face down on the burlap/hessian, leaving at least 3½ in (9 cm) between the frame and the edge of the burlap.

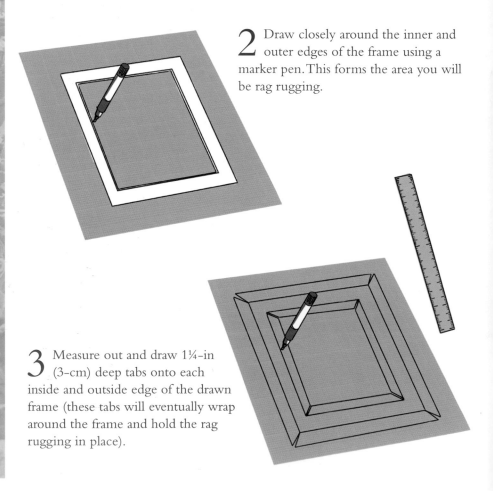

2 Draw closely around the inner and outer edges of the frame using a marker pen. This forms the area you will be rag rugging.

3 Measure out and draw 1¼-in (3-cm) deep tabs onto each inside and outside edge of the drawn frame (these tabs will eventually wrap around the frame and hold the rag rugging in place).

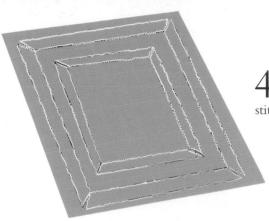

4 Use the sewing machine to hem along all the lines using one row of placeholder hemming stitch (see page 13). Cut off any loose threads.

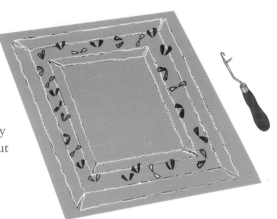

5 Cut your fabric into short strips for shaggy rag rugging using the gauge (see pages 13–15). Shaggy rag rug (see pages 21–22) inside the hemmed frame (but not in the tabs). Keep rag rugging until no burlap can be seen from the front. You do not need to rag rug as tightly as normal, as the pieces will become secured against the frame.

6 Trim off any excess burlap from inside and outside the rag rugged frame using everyday scissors. Be careful not to cut off the inner or outer tabs you hemmed earlier.

7 Place the burlap shaggy side down and line up the frame with the rag rugging. Fold the burlap tabs over the frame and secure in place using the staple gun. When securing the inside tabs, make sure they are stapled to the part of the frame where the backing board will sit. The thickness of the burlap will compensate for the thickness lost by removing the glass.

8 To make the chalkboard, place the backing board from the frame face up on old newspaper. Paint the front of the backing board with one coat of chalkboard paint. Let it dry for an hour, then apply another coat.

9 When the paint is completely dry, put the chalkboard into the frame and secure it in place with the metal tabs on the back of the frame. If any of the shaggy pieces of fabric are obstructing the chalkboard too much, trim them to a slightly shorter length.

NAUTICAL PILLOW

Cool blues and grays are always popular as they fit into almost any interior color scheme, and the varied widths of the stripes in this pillow make for an interesting and sophisticated design. I love the way the fraying of the cotton gives a slightly distressed appearance, the rough edges reminding us that these projects are all about upcycling something that has lost its primary usefulness.

1 Use the marker pen to draw a 16 x 16-in (40 x 40-cm) square on the burlap/hessian, making sure to leave at least 3¼ in (8 cm) between each side of the square and the edge of the burlap. Draw a second square 1½ in (4 cm) outside the first square. Stitch along the four sides of the inner and outer squares using one row of placeholder hemming stitch (see page 13).

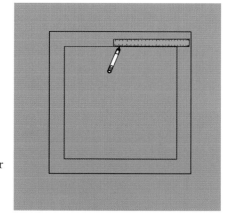

2 Cut the shirts into long strips for loopy rag rugging (see pages 13–14). You will need at least six men's shirts for this project.

3 This pillow has stripes of varying widths. Loopy rag rug (see pages 18–19) the inner square following the pattern on the right. Start by rag rugging along the top inside edge of the pillow, keeping as close to the hemming as possible. Leave two or three rows of holes in the burlap between each row of rag rugging. Once the pillow is entirely rag rugged, cut away any excess burlap around the outer hemmed square.

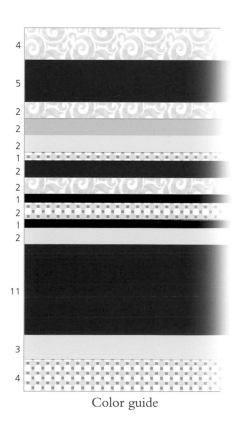

Color guide

YOU WILL NEED

Burlap/hessian

Marker pen

Tape measure or ruler

Sewing machine and thread

Assorted fabrics (I used six men's shirts)

Fabric scissors

Latch hook

Everyday scissors

Tailors' chalk or pencil

Backing fabric
(I recommend thick cotton)

Pins

Iron

Zipper foot (optional)

16 x 16-in (40 x 40-cm) pillow form/
cushion pad

2 large buttons

Needle and thread

COLOR PALETTE

Checked and striped men's shirts in blue, green, gray, and neutral

4 Cut out two rectangles of fabric each measuring 19 x 14 in (48 x 36 cm) for the back of the pillow. It helps to mark the pieces out using tailors' chalk or a pencil before cutting them out.

5 Hem along one of the longer edges of each backing piece. Do this by folding the raw edge over twice by about ½ in (1 cm), then press with an iron. Pin if needed, then machine stitch in place using straight stitch. Cut off any loose threads and press both pieces of fabric.

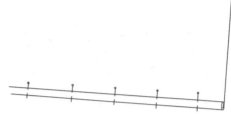

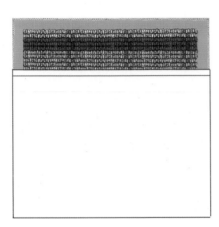

6 Place your rag rugged square face up on a table. Lay one of the backing pieces on top of the square. The hemmed edge should be nearest the center of the pillow and the rough side of the hemming should be facing up.

7 Place your second backing piece on the pillow. As before, the hemmed edge should be nearest the center of the pillow and the rough side of the hemming should be facing up. The backing pieces will overlap near the center of the pillow.

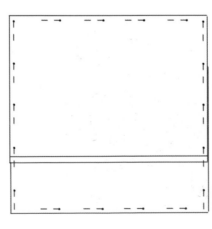

8 Pin the layers in place. Pin as close to the rag rugging as possible, but try not to trap any of the rag rug loops or you will end up sewing over them.

TIP

YOU CAN ADAPT THESE
INSTRUCTIONS TO ANY SIZE
OF PILLOW, BUT IT IS EASIEST
TO CHOOSE STANDARD PILLOW
SIZES SO YOU CAN BUY
A FORM/PAD EASILY.

9 If you have a zipper foot for the sewing machine, now is the time to use it as it helps you to stitch a little closer to the rag rugging, giving a neater finish. Machine stitch all around the pillow using straight stitch. Stay as close to the rag rugging as possible.

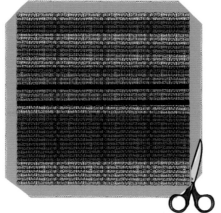

10 You now have a fully sewn-up pillow cover, but before you turn it right side out, diagonally cut off all the corners (being careful not to cut any stitches) and trim away some of the excess burlap and backing fabric from around the edge of the cover. This will remove some of the bulk from inside the pillow.

11 Turn the pillow cover right side out and insert the pillow form/ cushion pad. Sew two buttons to the back of the cover for extra detailing.

DEEP BLUE POUFFE

Pouffes are a great way to add extra seating to a living room without the need for bulky furniture. They're easy to move around and can be wonderfully comfy. With this project, I find that a simple color palette works best—the texture of the pouffe cover is so touchy-feely that it does most of the work for you. I've used a selection of blue fabrics ranging from deep royal blue to dark navy, but you can easily change the color scheme to one that suits your room.

YOU WILL NEED

Circular pouffe

Burlap/hessian—one piece for the top of the pouffe and another piece for the sides

Marker pen

Sewing machine and thread

Tape measure

Everyday scissors

Pins

Template (see page 123)

Assorted fabrics

Fabric scissors

Gauge

Latch hook

Needle and thread

Rag rug spring tool

COLOR PALETTE

Midnight blue, royal blue, navy

1 Place the pouffe upside down on the first piece of burlap/hessian. The pouffe should fit comfortably on the burlap and have a buffer of at least 3½ in (9 cm) all around. Draw around the pouffe using a marker pen.

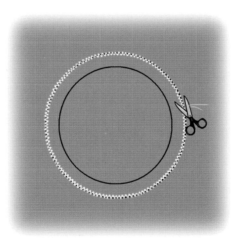

2 Draw a second circle 1½ in (4 cm) outside the first circle. Hem twice around the second circle using placeholder hemming stitch (see page 13) to create a secure border. Cut off any loose threads.

3 For the sides of the pouffe, measure the circumference of the pouffe at its widest point and make a note of the measurement. Measure the height of the pouffe and make a note of the measurement.

TIP

IF YOU DON'T HAVE A FLEXIBLE TAPE MEASURE, HOLD A PIECE OF STRING AROUND THE OUTSIDE OF THE POUFFE. MAKE A MARK ON THE STRING WHERE THE LOOSE END MEETS THE BEGINNING OF THE STRING, THEN MEASURE THAT DISTANCE USING A TAPE MEASURE OR RULER.

4 On the second piece of burlap, draw a rectangle the height of your pouffe + 1½ in (4 cm) x the circumference of your pouffe + 2 in (5 cm). Leave at least 2 in (5 cm) between the rectangle and the edge of the burlap.

5 Hem once around the rectangle using placeholder hemming stitch (see page 13). Cut off any loose threads. Use everyday scissors to cut away the excess burlap from one long edge of the rectangle. Do not cut away the burlap from any of the other edges of the rectangle.

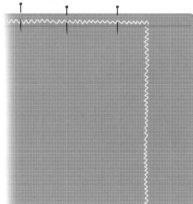

6 Fold the long edge that you have just trimmed over by ½ in (1 cm), pin, then secure in place using straight stitch (see edge hemming by machine, page 12). This will form the hemmed bottom edge of the pouffe.

7 Use the template on page 123 to draw tabs along the other long edge of the rectangle. The tabs should be ½ in (1 cm) apart. Don't worry if you end up with only half a tab at the end of the rectangle. Using placeholder hemming stitch (see page 13), sew along the tabs. The tabs will be used to join the sides of the pouffe cover to the top.

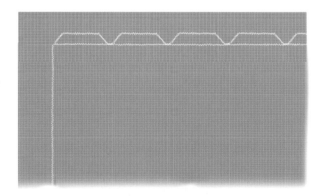

8 Trim the excess burlap from around the three untrimmed sides of the rectangle, making sure not to snip any of the stitches or accidentally cut the tabs off the long edge.

9 With the rough side of the bottom hem face down, fold the burlap so the two short sides meet. Line the two ends up and pin the edges together. Machine stitch together using straight stitch, ½ in (1 cm) from the edge. Turn the "cylinder" inside out (so that the seam is on the inside) and you are ready to rag rug.

10 Cut your fabric into short strips for shaggy rag rugging (see pages 13–15). Shaggy rag rug (see pages 21–22) inside the inner circle for the top of your pouffe, remembering that there should still be bare burlap between the rag rugged circle and the outer hemmed edge.

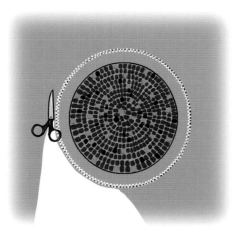

11 Carefully cut away the excess burlap from around the hemming, making sure not to snip any shaggy pieces of fabric or the stitching.

12 Now rag rug the sides of the pouffe. Shaggy rag rug (see pages 21–22) all the way around the cylinder of burlap except for the tabs at the top and the double-thickness hem at the bottom (this will be covered by the rag rugging above it). Try to rag rug as close to the vertical seam as possible, to hide the join.

13 Now join the pouffe together. Place the rag rugged cylinder and the rag rugged top on the pouffe so that they are in position. Pin the tabs of the cylinder to the burlap surrounding the top circle of the pouffe. The tabs should be overlaid on top. Baste/tack in place using a needle and thread.

14 Use the rag rug spring tool (see page 23) to rag rug through both layers of the burlap (i.e. the tabs and burlap surrounding the top of the pouffe) to join the pieces together. Keep adding fabric strips until the join is no longer visible and the pouffe cover feels secure.

PINK POSY PILLOW

Few things are more appealing after a long, hard day than sinking into a pile of soft, squishy pillows on a bed or sofa. For cushiness and comfort, you can't really beat a shaggy rag rug pillow, which is why I have them all around my apartment. They work well as single statement pieces on armchairs or can be layered together to create a cozy area. I have used shades of pink for this pillow, but you can adapt the pattern to fit any color scheme you would like.

YOU WILL NEED

Burlap/hessian

Marker pen

Tape measure or ruler

Sewing machine and thread

Everyday scissors

Assorted fabrics

Fabric scissors

Gauge

Latch hook

Tailors' chalk or pencil

Backing fabric (I recommend thick cotton)

Pins

Iron

Sticky tape

Zipper foot (optional)

16 x 16 in (40 x 40 cm) pillow form/cushion pad

COLOR PALETTE

Pinks, with the occasional row of light blue or purple (patterned fabrics work well)

1 Measure, mark, and hem the burlap/hessian by following step 1 of the Nautical Pillow on page 63.

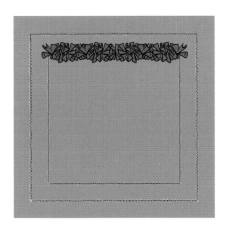

2 Cut your first pink fabric into short strips for shaggy rag rugging using fabric scissors and the gauge (see pages 13–15). Shaggy rag rug (see page 21–22) one row along one of the inside edges of the inner hemmed square, keeping as close to the hemming as possible (it doesn't matter which edge you choose).

3 Continue rag rugging one shaggy row after another, leaving two or three rows of holes in the burlap between each rag rugged row. Once the pillow is entirely rag rugged, cut away any excess burlap from around the larger hemmed square.

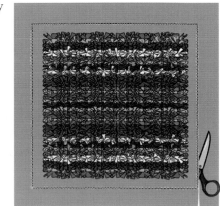

4 Following steps 4–5 of the Nautical Pillow on page 64, mark and cut out two pieces of backing fabric, each measuring 21½ x 14 in (55 x 36 cm)—they are larger in this project because shaggy rag rugging adds a lot of bulk to the pillow cover.

5 Working your way all around the four sides of the rag rugged square, tape back the shaggy fabric pieces so they won't get in the way when you are sewing your backing pieces to the hessian. You should be able to clearly see the inner hemming line just outside the rag rugging.

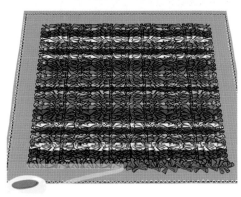

6 Once all the shaggy pieces are taped out of the way, place your rag rugged square face up on a table (I lay my rag rugging so that the lines are running horizontally). Follow steps 6–11 of the Nautical Pillow on page 65 to attach the back of the pillow cover.

7 Turn the pillow cover right side out and carefully remove the sticky tape from around the edges. Be gentle when doing this and hold the fabric pieces in place so that they do not get pulled out. Insert the pillow form/cushion pad.

BRAIDED COASTERS

Coasters always seem to be in short supply in my home. Whether they've migrated upstairs after a cup of tea in bed or found their way into the kitchen, I can never seem to find one when I need one. Braided/plaited coasters can be made in about half an hour and are great for protecting your tables and work surfaces.

YOU WILL NEED

Assorted fabrics

Fabric scissors

Bag clip or clothespin/peg

Tape measure or ruler

Sewing machine or needle and thread

Thread to match the fabric

COLOR PALETTE

Any fabric printed with a small pattern—I like using women's cotton shirts

TIP

THESE COASTERS CAN ALSO BE ASSEMBLED BY HAND USING A NEEDLE AND THREAD. FOR THIS METHOD, SEE THE BRAIDED RUG ON PAGES 48–50.

1 Turn your fabric into fabric yarn (see page 17). Cut the fabric yarn into three equal length strips. Measure 2½ in (6 cm) from the end of each of the strips and cut diagonally to the end of the strip to form a point.

2 Tie the pointed ends of the strips together tightly to form a small knot. Weigh down the knot under something (such as a hardback book) to make the braiding easier.

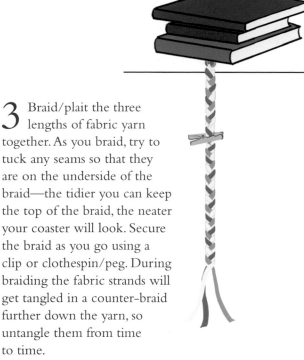

3 Braid/plait the three lengths of fabric yarn together. As you braid, try to tuck any seams so that they are on the underside of the braid—the tidier you can keep the top of the braid, the neater your coaster will look. Secure the braid as you go using a clip or clothespin/peg. During braiding the fabric strands will get tangled in a counter-braid further down the yarn, so untangle them from time to time.

4 Occasionally wind your braid in a rough circle to get an idea of how big your coaster will be. Secure the braid with a clip when you are happy with the size. Do not cut off the unbraided yarn at this stage in case you need to braid a little more.

5 Trim the ends from the knot at the beginning of the braid. Wind the braid into a circle, holding the inner edge of the braid tight to the knot. Sew the knot to the braid using placeholder hemming stitch (see page 13). Continue winding the braid loosely around in a circle, sewing the edges of the braid together with the zig zag stitch as you go. Make sure you feed the braid loosely under the sewing machine foot to prevent the coaster from curling up like a bowl. Continue until the coaster is the desired size.

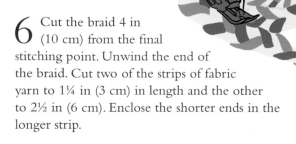

6 Cut the braid 4 in (10 cm) from the final stitching point. Unwind the end of the braid. Cut two of the strips of fabric yarn to 1¼ in (3 cm) in length and the other to 2½ in (6 cm). Enclose the shorter ends in the longer strip.

7 Sew the end of the strips to the edge of the coaster as if it was still a braid. You may need to use scissor blades to push the very end of the fabric strip right up to the edge of the coaster to create a smooth edge.

BOHEMIAN STOOL

This shaggy seat cover is a fun way to give an old stool a new lease on life. The best stool for this project is one that has screws underneath with a seat that lifts off so you can work on it separately. This cover is inspired by the "boucherouite" rag rugs of Morocco—diamond patterns feature heavily in their designs, as well as bright colors that pop against neutral backgrounds. I may be a little over-imaginative, but with its four legs and cream background this stool reminds me of a little shaggy sheep!

YOU WILL NEED

Stool with detachable seat pad

Screwdriver

Burlap/hessian

Marker pen

Tape measure or ruler

Sewing machine and thread

Template on page 123

Assorted fabrics

Fabric scissors

Gauge

Latch hook

Everyday scissors

Staple gun

Backing fabric (e.g. cotton)

COLOR PALETTE

Black, lilac, light pink, light yellow, coral, cream

1 Turn the stool upside down and unscrew the seat pad from the base of the stool. Make sure you keep all the screws together in a safe place so that you can easily assemble it again.

2 Place the seat pad face down on the burlap/hessian and draw around it with a marker pen. Leave at least 12 in (30 cm) between the edge of the seat pad and the edge of the burlap. The shape you have drawn will be the top of your rag rug stool.

3 Measure the depth of the seat pad. Draw tabs on each side of the square to the depth of the seat pad. Creating these tabs will ensure that the sides of the stool are fully rag rugged, too. The tabs are split at the corners to allow them to fit around the seat pad without any excess burlap getting in the way.

TIP

MIX YOUR CREAM FABRICS WELL AS YOU RAG RUG THE BACKGROUND OF THE STOOL. THERE ARE MANY DIFFERENT SHADES OF CREAM AND BLENDING HELPS YOU AVOID OBVIOUS BLOCKS OF ONE FABRIC.

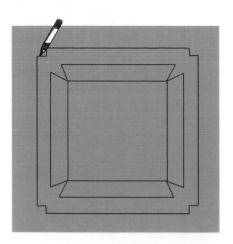

4 Draw a hem around the edge of the seat pad and tabs, approximately 3¼ in (8 cm) from the edge of the tabs.

5 Sew along all the lines using placeholder hemming stitch (page 13). Use thread to match the background color of your rag rugging, so that it will be hidden amongst the fabric strips (I used cream thread).

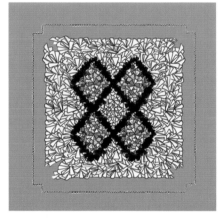

6 Create the diamond pattern on the seat pad by drawing around the template on page 123. If your stool is small and the template does not fit or if you would like the diamonds to stretch fully across your seat pad, you can adapt the pattern to any size.

7 Cut the black fabric into short strips for shaggy rag rugging using fabric scissors and the gauge (see pages 13–15). Shaggy rag rug (see pages 21–22) one row around the edge of each of the diamonds. Fill in each of the diamonds in a mixture of lilac, light pink, and light yellow fabric. Add in a few random pieces of coral fabric to add depth to the design.

8 Fill in the rest of the square and the side tabs of the seat pad in cream shaggy rag rugging. Do not rag rug the outer hemmed border.

9 When the seat pad and side tabs are fully rag rugged, cut away any excess burlap from around the outer hemming. Lay the burlap with the rag rugging face down and place the seat pad face down on top, aligning the pad with the rag rugged square. Fold the outer burlap border onto the seat pad and secure to the base using the staple gun, being careful not to obstruct the holes where the stool screws go in. You will need to pleat the burlap at the corners.

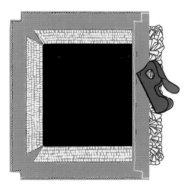

10 Cut a piece of backing fabric 1½ in (4 cm) wider and longer than the seat pad. Staple this to the back of the seat pad, folding the raw edge of the backing fabric underneath to hide it. Make small holes in the backing fabric where the screw holes are, then screw the seat pad back onto the stool base.

COZY DRAFT EXCLUDER

If, like me, you've lived in an old house, you probably understand when I say how drafty they can get. Antique doors and single glazing definitely don't make for great insulation! A draft excluder is amazingly effective, and the layers and amount of fabric used in shaggy rag rugging makes it incredibly insulating and perfect for keeping out unwelcome gusts of wind.

1 Measure the width of your door excluding the doorframe (this will be the length of your draft excluder). Draw a rectangle onto the burlap/hessian. It should be the width of your door by 12 in (30 cm) high. Leave at least 2 in (5 cm) between the rectangle and the edge of the burlap.

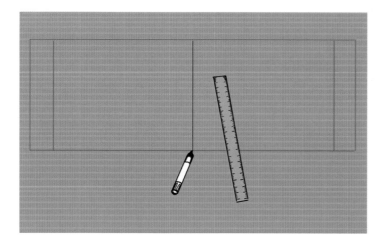

2 On both sides of the burlap (front and back), draw a vertical line 1½ in (4 cm) in from each short end. Also draw a vertical line down the center of the rectangle. (It is easiest to use a marker pen to draw fairly thick lines on one side of the burlap first, then turn it over and you will be able to see these lines through the holes in the weave. You can then draw on top of these lines of the second side of the burlap.)

3 Machine stitch once around the rectangle using placeholder hemming stitch (see page 13), then cut away any excess burlap from around the rectangle, making sure not to cut through the stitching.

YOU WILL NEED

Tape measure

Burlap/hessian

Marker pen

Everyday scissors

¾-in (2-cm) wide sew-on Velcro (hook-and-loop tape), enough for the width of your door

Pins

Sewing machine, needle, and thread

40 in (1 m) grosgrain ribbon, ¾ in (2 cm) wide (color matched)

Duct tape

Assorted fabrics

Fabric scissors

Gauge

Latch hook

Filling (such as cut-up rags or polyester batting/wadding)

Rag rug spring tool

COLOR PALETTE

Lilac, gray, light blue, with accent tartan

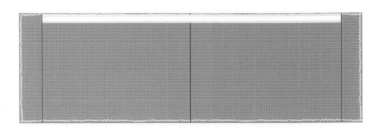

4 Pin the "loop" part of the Velcro to one long edge of the
rectangle, positioning the Velcro between the drawn lines at
each end of the rectangle. Cut to the correct length if necessary.
Machine stitch along both edges of the Velcro with straight stitch
to secure it to the burlap.

5 Turn the burlap over and pin the ribbon to
the burlap behind the Velcro. Cut to length and
tuck the ends of the ribbon under themselves for a
neat finish. Machine stitch along both edges of the
ribbon with straight stitch to secure it to the back
of the Velcro.

6 Machine stitch the "hook" length of Velcro to the
other long edge of the rectangle (on the same side
of the burlap as the ribbon), using straight stitch on each
edge. The side of the burlap with the ribbon is the side
you will be rag rugging. Cover both pieces of Velcro
with duct tape to prevent them from getting fuzzy
during the rag rugging stage.

7 Prepare your first fabric for shaggy rag rugging
by cutting it into short pieces using the gauge
(see pages 13–15). Shaggy rag rug (see pages 21–22)
your first row along the central line drawn on the
burlap. Remember: the ribbon is on the side you are
rag rugging (here the ribbon is shown in green and
the duct tape in black).

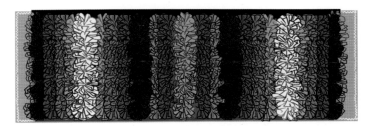

8 Choose your next fabric and rag rug one row to the
left and one row to the right of the first central row.
Continue rag rugging in this pattern, working evenly on
the left and then the right, until you reach the lines drawn
1½ in (4 cm) from each end of the rectangle.

9 Remove the duct tape from the Velcro. Stick the
Velcro together to make the draft excluder into
a tube (the ends should still be open). Push as much
filling in as possible, making sure the tube is evenly
filled all the way along.

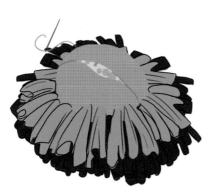

10 Sew the ends of the draft excluder together by folding the zig zag stitching inside and overcast stitching the two pieces of burlap together.

11 Use the rag rug spring tool (see page 23) to continue rag rugging one row at each end of the draft excluder at a time (as you've been doing before, to keep the pattern consistent) until you have covered both ends of the draft excluder and no burlap is visible. Open up the Velcro and add in more filling if needed.

FOLK ART WALL HANGING

Rag rugging is a surprisingly versatile craft and once you have gained confidence, you can create very intricate pictures. Kaffe Fassett is a great fan of the medium and has created some true pictorial masterpieces out of rags alone. Here I have used short, compact loops to depict an abstract countryside scene with tall poplar trees and a little house perched on a hill. The patchwork of brightly colored fields at the bottom of the wall hanging is a great place to use up small scraps of fabric. I recommend trying a couple of other rag rug projects before embarking on this one as it is slightly more challenging, particularly for a rag rug novice.

YOU WILL NEED

Burlap/hessian

Tape measure

Marker pen

Everyday scissors

Sewing machine or needle and thread

Wooden pole (I used a bamboo cane from the garden center, cut to size using a saw)

Pins

Ruler

Template on page 123

Latch hook

Assorted fabrics

Fabric scissors

Pencil

Twine (I used bakers' twine)

COLOR PALETTE

A real mixture

1 Cut and edge hem (see pages 11–12) a burlap/hessian rectangle measuring 24 x 20 in (60 x 50 cm). This can be done by either machine or hand sewing. Try to keep in line with the weave of the burlap as much as possible (see page 10).

2 Lay the rectangle with the rough side of the hemming face up. Place the wooden pole across one of the short sides of the rectangle and fold the burlap over the pole. The pole should fit comfortably under the folded-over burlap. Make a mark at each side of the rectangle where the fold reached, then use the marker pen to draw a line to connect the two marks. Try to keep the drawn line parallel with the weave of the burlap so that your wall hanging will hang straight (see page 10).

3 Set the pole aside. Pin the burlap fold and sew along the edge to create a channel for the pole to fit in comfortably. Once sewn, check that the pole will easily slide through the channel. If the pole does not fit, you will need to unpick the tube and start again.

4 Now you are ready to draw your design onto the burlap using the marker pen. Copy the template from page 123. Start by drawing the two hills, then add the house to the top of the hill on the right. Sketch in the vertical lines between the fields, then add the horizontal lines—it doesn't matter exactly where these are, so feel free to put in more lines to create more fields or remove lines to create bigger blocks. Add the sun to the top left corner, then draw in the three trees and the bush.

5 Cut your fabrics for loopy rag rugging (see pages 13–14). Cut your strips approximately ½ in (1 cm) wide to create a more detailed piece.

6 Loopy rag rug (see pages 18–19) along all the lines of the fields using black, navy, or dark gray. I used a mixture of all three colors to use up little scraps I had lying around. Your loops should be less than ½ in (1 cm) in height to create a finer design.

7 Loopy rag rug to fill in each of the fields using different colors and patterns. I used a mixture of blocks of patterned fabrics, striped designs, and random rag rugged sections. There is no right or wrong way to rag rug them, but I began with the left hill and worked my way across to the right. I repeated certain fabrics to give the impression of some fields having the same crops. Try to avoid yellows, as these would blend in too much with the sky.

8 I used three shades of brown for the tree trunks. Use the darkest brown to rag rug a row up the right side of each tree trunk. Rag rug one row using the medium shade of brown on the left of the first row. Finally, rag rug using the lightest shade of brown on the left of both rows. This graduation of color creates the impression of light from the sun hitting one side of the tree and shading the other side.

9 Beginning with the tree in the middle, loopy rag rug the outline of the tops of the three trees using different shades of green. I used a darker shade of green for the tree in the middle to create contrast between the trees. Loopy rag rug five red berries onto the tree on the left—it doesn't matter where they are placed. The berries consist of only one loop. Fill in the rest of the tree on the left using different shades of bottle green. Randomly rag rug to create an interesting pattern within the tree itself.

10 Loopy rag rug a wiggly line up the middle tree using light green, then fill in the rest of the tree in dark green. Loopy rag rug flowers onto the tree on the right using a sparkly fabric. I used sari fabric that features sequins and beading for extra texture. Fill in the rest of the tree using different shades of green.

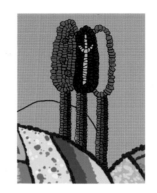

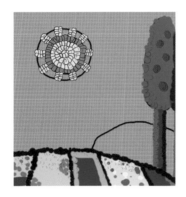

11 Using a bright shade of yellow, loopy rag rug around the inner circle of the sun and fill in with the same shade of yellow. Change to orange and rug a row around the outside of the circle. Use the inner yellow fabric to loopy rag rug the rays coming out of the sun. These should be two rows wide and extend to the outer circle, approximately ¾ in (2 cm) away.

12 Loopy rag rug the edge of the hedge in a bright green. Fill in the hedge by randomly rag rugging in different shades of light and bright green.

13 Rag rug the edge of the left house using a deep orange fabric (I tried to match a brick color). By rag rugging the edge of the house first, you get a good idea of how much space you have for the windows. Loopy rag rug one row in white around the edges of all the windows and the door. Rag rug a white cross in the center of each of the windows on the left side of the house and one horizontal line across the center of each of the windows on the right side of the house. Fill in the rest of the windows using black. Rag rug the porch in black.

14 Loopy rag rug the roofs of both parts of the house in a black-and-white patterned fabric. Rag rug the two chimneys in deep red. Fill in the left part of the house in deep orange rag rugging and the right part of the house and the door in teal.

15 Cut four shades of light yellow fabric into long strips and, starting at the top of the hills, loopy rag rug the remaining burlap up to the stitching at the top of the wall hanging. Mix the shades of yellow well to add complexity to your design.

16 Place the pole into the channel and measure so that there is 1¼ in (3 cm) sticking out at each end of the hessian. Make a mark using a pencil and cut down to size if necessary. To hang up your wall hanging, tie twine to each end of the pole, as close to the burlap as possible. Tuck the knots into the channel for a tidier look.

TEATIME TRIVET

A trivet is one of the best projects for a rag rug beginner. It's a small, portable project that can be made in a couple of hours and, most importantly, it gives you the chance to practice both loopy and shaggy rag rugging techniques.

1 Place the plate upside down on the burlap/hessian and draw around it with the marker pen. Make sure you leave at least 2 in (5 cm) between the circle and the edge of the burlap/hessian.

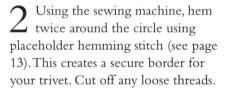

2 Using the sewing machine, hem twice around the circle using placeholder hemming stitch (see page 13). This creates a secure border for your trivet. Cut off any loose threads.

3 Cut the fabric for the shaggy border into short strips using the gauge (see pages 13–15). Cut your other fabric into long strips for loopy rag rugging (see pages 13–14).

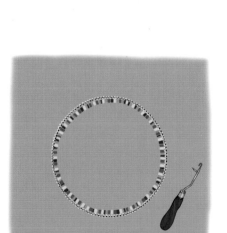

4 Shaggy rag rug (see pages 21–22) just inside the hemmed circle of the trivet. Try to get as close to the hemming as possible, as shown above from the back of the burlap.

5 Change to the second fabric and loopy rag rug (see pages 18–19) around the inside of the shaggy border. I rag rug in concentric rings toward the center of the trivet until it is fully rag rugged, but you can work in rows if you find it easier.

6 Cut carefully around the trivet using everyday scissors, cutting as close to the hemming as possible without snipping the stitches. Do not use fabric scissors as the hessian will blunt them. As you cut the burlap, take care not to snip the shaggy outer border—it's very annoying if you accidentally do this!

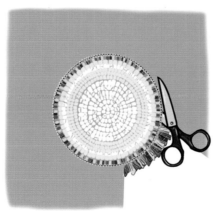

TIP

IF THE SHAGGY BORDER OF YOUR TRIVET IS LOOKING A BIT WILD, TRIM THE ENDS SO THEY ARE ALL SLIGHTLY SHORTER AND THE SAME LENGTH. THIS WILL GIVE A MORE POLISHED LOOK.

"SHOP 'TIL YOU DROP" TOTE

These bright and breezy bags are not only excellent for little shopping excursions but will undoubtedly bring a smile to your face. There are limitless possibilities for designs, but here I've included two very simple yet effective motifs to get you started. You can also do your own take on these by creating different varieties or colors of flowers or cats.

YOU WILL NEED

Templates on page 123

Unlaminated burlap/hessian bag (see tip)

Marker pen

Ruler

Assorted fabrics

Fabric scissors

Latch hook

COLOR PALETTE

For the cat: black

For the flower: 3 shades of yellow, 3 shades of green, hot pink

CAT DESIGN

1 Photocopy or trace the template on page 123, cut it out, and draw around it on the bag using the marker pen.

TIP

CHECK THAT YOUR BAG IS UNLAMINATED, I.E. THAT THE INSIDE OF THE BAG IS NOT COATED WITH A PLASTIC FILM. IF THE BAG IS LAMINATED, RAG RUGGING THROUGH IT WILL BE REALLY DIFFICULT.

2 Cut your black fabric in to long strips for loopy rag rugging (see pages 13–14), cutting strips ½ in (1 cm) wide and as long as possible. Loopy rag rug (see pages 18–19) around the edge of the cat, then fill it in. All your loops should be less than ½ in (1 cm) in height to create a more defined pattern.

FLOWER DESIGN

1 Use a marker pen to draw a 2¼-in (6-cm) diameter circle on the bag wherever you would like the top of your flower to be. Either use the template on page 123 or draw around a small circular object.

2 For the stem draw a 4-in (10-cm) line down from the bottom of the circle using a ruler. Using the leaf templates on page 123, draw two leaves on the stem, one at the bottom right of the stem and one 1½ in (4 cm) up the stem on the left.

3 Prepare your fabric for loopy rag rugging (see pages 13–14). As burlap/hessian bags tend to have a tighter weave, it helps to cut strips slightly narrower than normal—around ½ in (1 cm) wide—to make the rag rugging a little easier.

4 Loopy rag rug (see pages 18–19) around the circle in your first yellow. All your loops should be less than ½ in (1 cm) in height to keep the design compact. Next, rag rug three concentric circles in alternating yellows, leaving an empty hessian circle in the center of the flower. Loopy rag rug the center of the flower in hot pink.

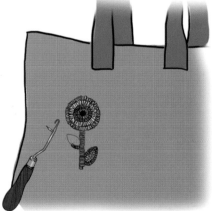

5 Loopy rag rug along the stem with one shade of green. Loopy rag rug along the outsides of the leaves in another shade of green, then fill in using the third shade of green.

FLOWER HAIR ACCESSORY

This gorgeous flower clip is the perfect project for using up and showcasing your favorite fabric offcuts. You know the ones—the small pieces of printed and patterned fabric that are too small to make much out of, but are too pretty to throw away. It makes a perfect spring or summer accessory, and you can make flowers in all different shapes and sizes once you know how.

YOU WILL NEED:

Small circular object, e.g. a large coin or the base of an egg cup, about 1¼ in (3 cm) in diameter

Burlap/hessian

Marker pen

Sewing machine and thread

Assorted fabrics

Fabric scissors

Gauge

Latch hook

Everyday scissors

2 x 2-in (5 x 5-cm) scrap of felt

Glue gun

Barrette/hair clip

COLOR PALETTE

Anything goes!

1 Leaving at least 2 in (5 cm) between the circle and the edge of the burlap/hessian, use the marker pen to draw a small circle on the burlap. Use the sewing machine to hem twice around the circle using placeholder hemming stitch (see page 13) to create a secure border. Cut off any loose threads.

2 Cut your fabric into short strips for shaggy rag rugging (see pages 13–15). I use at least three different fabrics for each flower, and you will need a maximum of 20 strips per fabric.

3 Choose the fabric for the outside of your flower. Use these strips to shaggy rag rug (see pages 21–22) just inside the circle, making sure to keep close to the stitching.

4 Choose your next fabric and shaggy rag rug in a circle around the inside of the rag rug border.

5 Fill in the center of your flower, shaggy rag rugging with your final fabric. The circle should now be fully rag rugged with no burlap visible from the front.

6 Trim the excess burlap from around the circle, making sure not to snip any of the stitches of the hemming or the rag rug pieces. This is best done with everyday scissors from the non-shaggy side of the burlap.

7 Cut a piece of felt slightly bigger than the burlap base of your flower, i.e. approximately 2 x 2 in (5 x 5 cm). Carefully attach the felt to the hessian base of the flower using the glue gun.

8 Once the glue has dried, carefully trim around the edge of the felt so that the burlap base of the flower is fully covered. Take care not to snip the rag rug pieces while doing this.

9 Use the glue gun to attach the flower to the top of a sturdy barrette/hair clip.

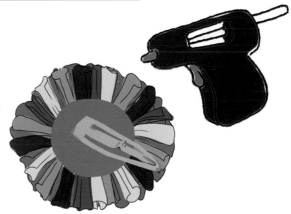

WATERMELON CLUTCH

The design for this lovely watermelon clutch bag was inspired by a recent trip to the sunny island of Aitutaki in the Cook Islands. I wanted to capture some of the flavor and feel of this Pacific Island paradise and could think of nothing more vibrant and iconic than a slice of juicy watermelon—it takes me right back to the beach! Although I made this as a casual clutch bag, you could use a waterproof material for the lining and use it as a wash bag.

YOU WILL NEED

12-in (30-cm) zipper

Everyday scissors

16 x 16 in (40 x 40 cm) backing fabric (see tip)

16 x 16 in (40 x 40 cm) burlap/hessian for front of clutch

32 x 32 in (80 x 80 cm) fabric for lining (see tip)

Marker pen

Sewing machine and thread

Fabric scissors

Iron

Ruler

Pins

Assorted fabrics

Latch hook

COLOR PALETTE

Dark and light green, white, dark and light coral, black, light blue, sky blue

1 Cut the large metal block off the non-zipper end of your zipper. IMPORTANT: do not unzip the zipper after doing this.

2 From your backing fabric, cut two small rectangles each 2½ in (6 cm) long and the width of your zipper (including the fabric strips either side of the zipper teeth). Place one rectangle face down so that the end aligns with the trimmed end of the zipper. Machine sew across the end of the zipper, using a straight stitch. Manually work the machine across the teeth of the zipper so that you do not break the needle. Cut off any loose threads.

3 Unzip the zipper slightly and place the second rectangle face down at the other end of the zipper. Use a straight stitch to sew it in place, making sure that the ends of the zipper beyond the zipper pull are firmly together. Once sewn, fold the tabs back on themselves.

-TIP-

CHOOSE A RELATIVELY THICK
FABRIC FOR THE BACK OF YOUR
CLUTCH TO COUNTERBALANCE THE
THICKNESS OF THE RAG RUGGING
ON THE FRONT. CHOOSE A THIN
FABRIC FOR THE LINING SO THAT
THINGS DON'T BECOME
TOO BULKY.

4 Mark out the front piece of the clutch on the burlap/hessian using a marker pen. The length of the bag should be the length of the zipper (including the attached rectangles) and the depth should be 8 in (20 cm). Sew along any sides of the burlap that are unhemmed using one row of placeholder hemming stitch (see page 13), then cut out the burlap rectangle.

5 Use the burlap rectangle as a template to cut out the back of the clutch bag from the backing fabric and two pieces for the lining of the clutch. These should all be the same size as the burlap rectangle.

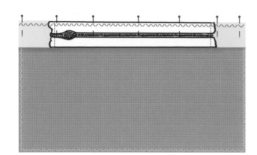

6 Place the zipper on the burlap rectangle, with the right side of the zipper facing down (any edge hemming should be face down). Pin and then sew along the edge of the zipper and burlap using zig zag stitch, all the way from one end of the fabric tab to the other. This will act as a holding stitch.

7 Sew a straight stitch along the top of the zig zag stitch closest to the zipper, touching the edge of the zig zag stitch. This secures everything tightly.

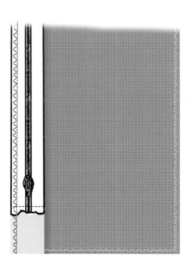

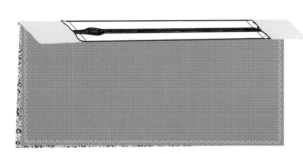

8 With the zipper face down and the stitching at the top of the zip, take one piece of lining and lay it on top of the zipper. The zipper should be sandwiched between the burlap and the lining. Align the long edge of the lining with the top of the zipper you have just sewn along. Pin and then zig zag stitch the lining to the top of the zipper, then sew a straight stitch along the bottom of the zig zag stitch (touching the bottom of the zig zag stitch as before).

9 Press the burlap and lining away from the zipper using an iron. Use a fairly low setting on the iron and be careful as the metal of the zipper can get very hot.

10 Lay out the partially constructed bag so that the zipper tab is facing upward. Place the backing fabric face down so that it aligns with the top of the zipper. Pin, then zig zag stitch the edge of the backing fabric to the top of the zipper, then do a line of straight stitch, touching the zig zag as before.

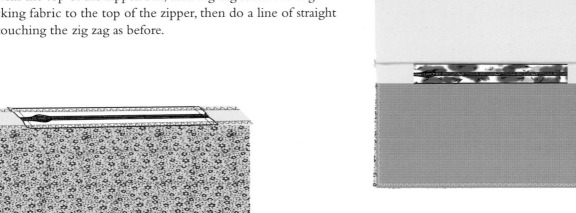

11 Lay the partially constructed clutch down so that the lining side is facing upward. All the other layers should be underneath and the zipper should be at the top. Place the second piece of lining face down to sandwich the zipper between the two layers of lining. The top of the detached piece of lining should be aligned with the top of the zipper. Pin, then zig zag stitch the lining to the zipper. Then straight stitch along the tops of the Vs of the zig zag stitch to tidy things up as before.

12 Press the fabric away from the zipper using an iron. This is best done from the lining side of the bag.

13 It is extremely important at this stage that you open your zipper. If you don't, you will not be able to turn the clutch the right way round later. Place the clutch so that the lining pieces are lined up together and the burlap and backing pieces are lined up together. Pinch together the small backing fabric rectangles at each end of the zipper and pin in place. Use straight stitch to sew together the backing fabric and burlap, making sure to sew the backing tabs into their pinned position. Go round the bottom corners in a smooth curve.

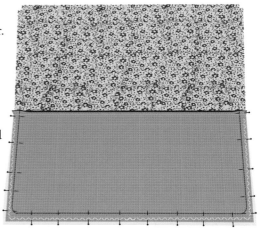

14 Carefully turn the clutch inside out by pushing the corners up through the open zipper. This will be the shape of your clutch, so if you're not happy with the shape of the corners, turn the clutch inside out again and re-sew.

15 Copy the watermelon template on page 127. Pin it in place on the burlap in the center of the clutch and draw around it. Remove the template and draw the inner curved line and the pips.

16 Cut your fabric into long strips for loopy rag rugging (see pages 13–14). Your strips should be as long as possible, but only about ½ in (1 cm) wide to allow for a more delicate picture.

17 Loopy rag rug (see pages 18–19) in dark green along the outside line of the watermelon. All your loops should be just under ½ in (1 cm) in height. Loopy rag rug a line of light green just inside, and then a line of white followed by a line of light coral. Rag rug the "pips" in black (these consist of only one loop between the ends of the strip). Fill in the remainder of the watermelon using dark coral.

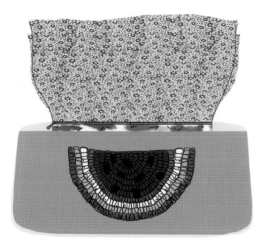

18 Loopy rag rug the light blue border of the clutch. This may be quite tricky in places, as you have to rag rug close to the join of the bag, but do try to get as close to the edge as possible. Fill in the rest of the hessian in sky blue loopy rag rugging. I rag rugged from the outside of the clutch inward, but you can do it in whatever order you would like.

19 Once everything is fully rag rugged, turn the clutch carefully inside out again. Being careful not to cut any of the stitches, cut away the bulk from around the curve of the corners.

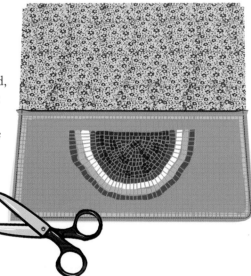

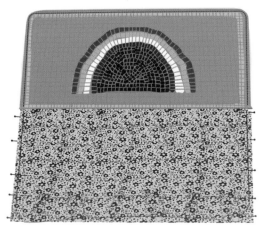

20 Pin, then stitch down the sides of the lining to attach them together. Make sure to round the corners slightly. Leave the bottom of the lining open or you will not be able to turn your bag inside out again.

21 Carefully turn the clutch inside out and pin the bottom of the lining fabrics together. Sew along the pinned edge, then push the lining back inside the clutch to finish.

ODDS AND ENDS CONTAINERS

If you're anything like me (and this tends to be true of many crafters), you probably have a treasure trove of crafty trinkets at home—buttons, threads, needles, offcuts of fabric, scissors… everything and anything that may "come in handy" at a later date. I am a true organization fiend—everything in my home has a place. These rag rug container covers are a great way of transforming everyday jars and tins into practical and beautiful storage, so there's no excuse for messy materials.

1 Measure the circumference of your jar using a flexible tape measure. Also measure the height of your jar. Make a note of both these measurements.

2 Draw a rectangle on the burlap/hessian that is the height of your container by the circumference + 1½ in (4 cm). Leave at least 2 in (5 cm) between the rectangle and the edge of the burlap. Draw a line ⅝ in (1.5 cm) inside the edge of each short end of the rectangle. Hem twice around the outside edge of the rectangle using placeholder hemming stitch (see page 13). Trim the excess burlap from each short end of the rectangle.

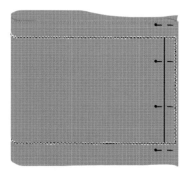

3 Pin the two short edges of the rectangle together, making sure that the hemming on the long edges aligns. This is extremely important or your container cover will end up crooked. Machine stitch along the drawn line using straight stitch, joining the short edges of the rectangle together.

YOU WILL NEED

Clean glass jar or metal tin

Flexible tape measure

Burlap/hessian

Marker pen

Ruler

Sewing machine and thread

Everyday scissors

Pins

Assorted fabrics

Fabric scissors

Latch hook

COLOR PALETTE

White, black, yellow (I used yellow sari silk for a rich look)

4 Turn the "tube" inside out, so the seam is on the inside. Place it over the jar to test that it fits comfortably. The rag rugging will add bulk, but trimming the seam (in step 8) will reduce bulk, so at this stage you need an approximate fit.

5 Prepare your fabric by cutting it into long strips for loopy rag rugging (see pages 13–14). Your strips should be approximately ½ in (1 cm) in width in order to create shorter, finer rag rug loops.

6 Loopy rag rug (see pages 18–19) one row of white fabric along one edge of the tube, keeping as close to the placeholder hemming as possible. You will need to have one of your hands inside the "tube" as you rag rug. Your loops should be fairly small—just under ½ in (1 cm) in height—to help create a defined pattern. Rag rug as close to the seam as possible in order to hide it.

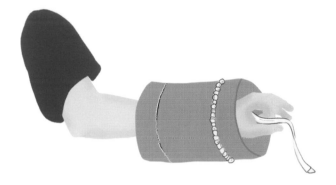

7 Continue rag rugging in rows up the length of the tube, alternating one row of white and one row of black. There should be approximately two empty rows of holes in the burlap between each rag rugged row and no burlap should be visible. When you have rag rugged half the tube, change to yellow fabric and continue rag rugging until you reach the placeholder hemming at the other end of the tube.

8 Carefully turn the tube inside out and trim away the excess burlap from the seam inside the tube, making sure not to cut any of the stitching.

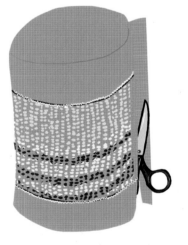

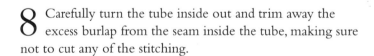

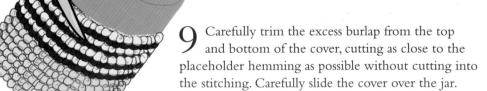

9 Carefully trim the excess burlap from the top and bottom of the cover, cutting as close to the placeholder hemming as possible without cutting into the stitching. Carefully slide the cover over the jar.

MAKING WAVES FRAMED ART

For me, art is one of the best tools to make a house into a home. It can dramatically transform a space and is a real reflection of your personality. Creating a piece of framed rag rug art is one of the simplest, yet most satisfying projects you can try when you're first starting out. Begin with a small frame and work your way up in size as you become more confident. I've used a very basic pattern here, but once you have mastered the loopy technique you can reproduce almost any artwork, no matter how complex.

YOU WILL NEED

Picture frame with mat mount (the frame should be at least ¾ in/2 cm deep)

Burlap/hessian

Marker pen

Ruler

Sewing machine and thread

Assorted fabrics

Fabric scissors

Latch hook

Everyday scissors

Sticky tape (optional)

COLOR PALETTE

Blues in different shades and fabrics

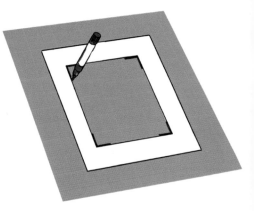

1 Remove the mat mount from the frame and place it face down onto the burlap/hessian, leaving at least 2¾ in (7 cm) between the mat and the edge of the burlap. Make sure you store the glass in a safe place where you won't break it. Taking care not to get pen marks on the mat, mark out where the inside corners of the mat are on the burlap.

2 Remove the mat and connect the corners together using a ruler and marker pen—this is the area you will be rag rugging. Measure out and draw a second rectangle 1 in (2.5 cm) outside the first one. Hem around this second line using placeholder hemming stitch (see page 13).

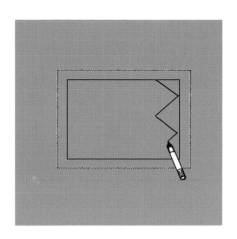

3 Draw a zig zag 1¼ in (3 cm) from one end of the drawn rectangle. The zig zag can have as many peaks as you would like.

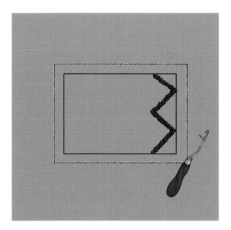

4 Prepare your fabric by cutting it into long strips for loopy rag rugging (see pages 13–14). The strips should be about ½ in (1 cm) wide to create a finer picture. Loopy rag rug (see pages 18–19) along the zig zag line with your first color, keeping the loops to just under ½ in (1 cm) in height.

TIP

IF THE RAG RUGGING IS NOT LYING CORRECTLY IN THE MOUNT, ATTACH THE BURLAP TIGHTLY TO THE BACK OF THE MOUNT WITH STICKY TAPE.

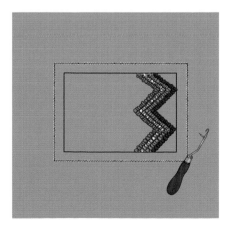

5 Take the fabric strips in the next color and rag rug following the line of the zig zag. Continue rag rugging, one fabric at a time, until you reach the end of the rectangle. Fill in the blank "triangles" at each end of the rectangle in loopy rag rugging to complete the art.

6 Trim the excess burlap from around the hemmed rectangle and place the rag rugged art in the mat. Place in the frame and put the backing board on. You can choose to put the glass in the frame or leave it open.

Chapter 3   FESTIVE

"SPRING IS IN THE AIR" BASKET

Wicker baskets make for pretty yet practical storage, so I have plenty in all different shapes and sizes in every room in my home. One day I was feeling particularly creative and decided to experiment by adding a rag rug trim to one of them. I liked it so much that I started to make my merry way through every basket I had, adding trims of different colors to each. This design is inspired by the fresh greens of spring and uses a number of different rag rug techniques. I can imagine filling it with chocolate for an Easter egg hunt.

YOU WILL NEED:

Wicker basket

Flexible tape measure

Burlap/hessian

Marker pen

Everyday scissors

Sewing machine and thread
(optional)

Needle and thread

Assorted fabrics

Fabric scissors

Latch hook

COLOR PALETTE

Black, cream, green

1 Measure the circumference around the top of the basket at its widest point, using a flexible tape measure. Draw a rectangle on the burlap/hessian that is the basket circumference + 2½ in (6 cm) by 4¾ in (12 cm) high. Hem all the edges of the burlap using either of the two edge hemming techniques (see pages 11–12). Cut off any loose threads.

2 Draw small circles approximately 4¾ in (12 cm) apart along the full length of the rectangle. It doesn't matter if these are slightly different shapes and sizes, as they are only a guide. These will form the centers of the flowers.

3 Cut the black fabric into long strips for loopy rag rugging (see pages 13–14). The strips should be approximately ½ in (1 cm) in width, as you will be rag rugging using short loops. Use the latch hook to rag rug eight short loops (see pages 18–19) to form a small black circle in the center of each of the marked circles. The loops should be less than ½ in (1 cm) in height.

4 Cut the cream fabric into long strips. The strips should be approximately ¾ in (2 cm) in width and as long as possible. Loopy rag rug (see pages 18–19) around the edge of the black rag rugging, keeping as close as possible. The loops and ends of strips should all be approximately 1¼–1½ in (3–4 cm) high to give a petal-like look.

5 Cut the green fabric into ¾-in (2-cm) strips for shaggy rag rugging (see pages 13–15). These strips are shorter than usual so that the flowers don't get swamped. Shaggy rag rug (see pages 21–22) between the flowers until the whole of the band is fully rag rugged.

TIP

IF YOUR FLOWERS ARE BEGINNING TO DISAPPEAR INTO THE "FOLIAGE," TRIM THE GREEN SHAGGY RAG RUGGING AROUND THE FLOWERS TO MAKE IT A BIT SHORTER. THIS WILL MAKE THE "FLOWERS" POP.

6 Hand sew the rag rugged band to the rim of the basket. Overlap the band slightly at the join for a seamless look.

FESTIVE WREATH

I love it when everyone starts crafting in the lead-up to Christmas… handmade cards, personalized presents, and decorations galore. This shaggy Christmas wreath is just the ticket for getting into the festive spirit. Rag rugging is a lovely craft to do in winter, as it makes you toasty warm. So put on your favorite Christmas sweater, get yourself a nice glass of mulled wine, and get rag rugging!

YOU WILL NEED

Template on page 126

¼-in (5-mm) thick foamboard (or cardboard—see tip)

Marker pen

Cutting mat

Scalpel

Burlap/hessian

Sewing machine and thread

Gold-colored candy wrappers

Assorted fabrics

Fabric scissors

Gauge

Latch hook

Everyday scissors

Staple gun

Burlap/hessian strands or ribbon, for hanging (optional)

Felt (optional)

Glue gun (optional)

COLOR PALETTE

Red, gold, green

1 To create the wreath base, copy the template from page 126 and use a marker pen to draw the ring onto the foamboard. Carefully cut out the ring using a scalpel and a sturdy cutting mat to protect your work surface. Don't worry if the edges of the ring are a little wiggly—they will not be on show.

2 Place the foamboard ring on the burlap/hessian, leaving at least 3½ in (9 cm) between the outside circle and the edge of the burlap. Draw around the inner and outer circles of the ring. The area between these lines is where you will be rag rugging.

TIP

IF YOU DO NOT HAVE FOAMBOARD, THICK CARDBOARD (OR LAYERS OF CARDBOARD GLUED TOGETHER) CAN BE USED AS AN ALTERNATIVE. THE CARDBOARD OR LAYERS MUST BE AT LEAST ¼ IN (5 MM) THICK OR THE WREATH WILL NOT HOLD ITS SHAPE.

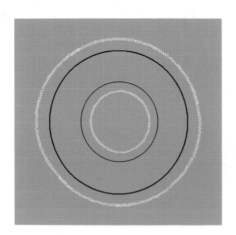

3 On the sewing machine, use placeholder hemming stitch (see page 13) to stitch two circles of hemming on the burlap. The first stitching line should be 1½ in (4 cm) outside the outer circle and the second should be 1½ in (4 cm) inside the inner circle of the wreath.

4 Use the marker pen to draw five small circles in the ring, equidistant from each other. These will become the five feature flowers of your wreath. Choose the material for the flower centers. It doesn't have to be fabric—I used gold candy wrappers for a glittering, festive look. Tightly shaggy rag rug (see pages 21–22) four pieces into each flower center.

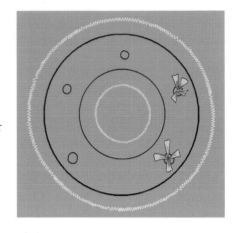

5 Using strips of red fabric, shaggy rag rug in circles again and again around the flower centers until your flowers reach the edge of the ring. Fill in the space between the flowers with varied shades of green fabric until all the burlap is covered and your wreath looks full. If the flowers in the wreath look squashed, remove some of the fabric strips from around them to give them space to spread out.

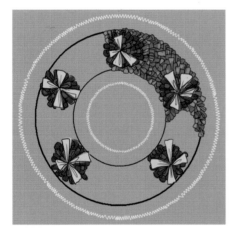

6 Cut around the outside hem to remove any excess burlap, being careful not to snip any stitches. This is best done from the non-shaggy side of the wreath. Then with the wreath shaggy side down, align the foamboard ring with the rag rugged wreath. Fold the burlap border over the foamboard ring and staple to secure (I find it easiest to staple four equidistant points, then fold and staple in between).

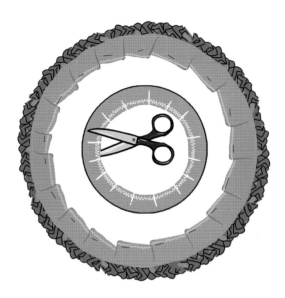

7 Cut out the inner circle of burlap. Make small, inward snips in the burlap to allow you to fold it in, making sure not to cut too close to the rag rugged part. Use the staple gun to secure the inside hem to the foamboard ring.

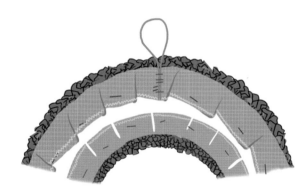

8 Add a hanging loop to the wreath. Braid/plait three burlap strands together and staple securely in a loop shape to the back of the wreath. If you wish, you could use twine, ribbon, or something more decorative.

9 If you're planning to give the wreath as a present or you just like things to be neat, tidy up the back of the wreath. Draw around the template on a piece of felt. Cut out the felt ring and glue it to the back of the wreath using a glue gun. Trim away any excess felt.

CHRISTMAS TREE BAUBLES

My cats have a field day when Christmas arrives and the decorations come out. They love to bat the vintage baubles off the Christmas tree (surely they're playthings after all?) and have broken dozens over the years. And so the rag rug bauble was born. Originally they occupied the lower branches as a way for the cats to continue to have their fun, but over the years they've made their way further up the tree to places of prominence.

YOU WILL NEED

Template on page 127

Cardboard for template

Burlap/hessian

Marker pen

Sewing machine and thread

Fabric scissors

Assorted fabrics

Gauge

Latch hook

Everyday scissors

Glue gun

Burlap/hessian strands or twine, three 6-in (15-cm) strands per bauble

COLOR PALETTE

Anything goes!

1 Copy the template from page 127 onto cardboard. Leaving at least 2 in (5 cm) between the edge of the burlap/hessian and the template, draw around the template using the marker pen. Use the sewing machine to hem twice around the template using placeholder hemming stitch (see page 13) to create a secure border. Cut off any loose threads.

2 Choose two fabrics for the bauble. Use your gauge and fabric scissors to cut your fabric into short strips for shaggy rag rugging (see pages 13–15).

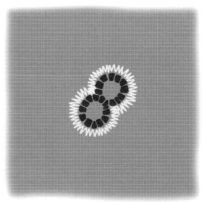

3 Using the fabric you have chosen for the outside of the bauble, shaggy rag rug (see pages 21–22) one row closely around the inside of the hemming. Make sure that the rag rugging meets in the center of the figure-eight shape (here the rag rugging is shown from the reverse side of the burlap).

4 Use your second fabric to fill in the rest of the shape, also using the shaggy technique. The shape should now be fully rag rugged, with no empty holes in the burlap.

TIP

USE OTHER MATERIALS FOR YOUR BAUBLES, SUCH AS RIBBON, CANDY WRAPPERS, AND SPARKLY FABRICS, FOR A FESTIVE LOOK.

5 Trim the excess burlap from around the hemming, making sure not to snip any of the stitches or the rag rug pieces. This is best done with everyday scissors from the non-shaggy side of the burlap.

6 To make the hanging loop, tie three strands of burlap or twine together in a knot at one end. Braid/plait the strands and tie a second knot at the bottom. Trim the ends if necessary.

7 Use the glue gun to glue the braid into a loop on the non-shaggy side of the rag rugging. Glue the bauble together by folding the figure-eight in half, sandwiching the loop between the two sides of the burlap. Fluff up the bauble and trim any ends that look out of place.

PASTEL BUNTING

Whether made for a celebration or as an all-year decoration, bunting is a wonderful way to bring a bit of color and festivity to the home. I love bunting of all different sizes and styles, but the texture of rag rug just adds that certain bit of *je ne sais quoi*. I've used pastel tones here, but you can use any colors under the sun.

YOU WILL NEED

Template on page 126

Cardboard for template

Burlap/hessian

Marker pen

Sewing machine and thread

Assorted fabrics (see tip on page 112)

Fabric scissors

Latch hook

Everyday scissors

3¼ yds (3 m) grosgrain ribbon, plus thread to match

Pins

Ruler

Sewing machine zipper foot (optional)

COLOR PALETTE

Pastel shades of yellow, green, blue, lilac, pink, orange

1 Copy the template from page 126 onto a piece of cardboard and cut it out. Place the template on the burlap/hessian, leaving at least 3¼ in (8 cm) between the frayed edge of the burlap and the template. Use a marker pen to draw around the template, and repeat eight times (or to create as many flags as you would like).

TIP

DON'T BE TEMPTED TO MAKE FLAGS THAT ARE MUCH LARGER THAN THE TEMPLATE, AS LARGER FLAGS BECOME QUITE HEAVY WHEN THEY ARE FULLY RAG RUGGED.

2 Following the template, draw a horizontal line to connect the two top corners of each flag. This separates the part of the burlap that will be rag rugged from the top tab that will be attached to the ribbon.

3 Use the sewing machine to hem twice along all the lines of all the flags using placeholder hemming stitch (see page 13). Cut off any loose threads.

4 Choose the two fabrics you would like to use for your first flag. Cut the fabric into long strips for loopy rag rugging (see pages 13–14).

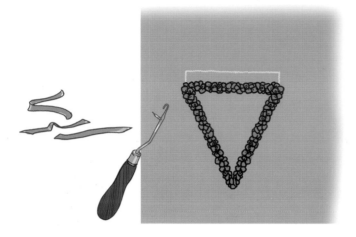

5 Using the main fabric for your first flag, loopy rag rug (see pages 18–19) all around the inside edge of the triangle, keeping as close to the stitching as possible.

6 Change to your second color and loopy rag rug around the inside of the rag rugged triangle, keeping as close as possible to the first row of rag rugging.

7 Change back to your original fabric and fill the inside of the triangle with loopy rag rugging. I do this by rag rugging in smaller and smaller concentric triangles until I reach the center, but you can do this however you wish. After your second row of rag rugging you do not need to rag rug the rows as close together—rag rug close enough that the burlap does not show from the front, but sufficiently far apart that the loops have some space to spread out (see page 20). Rag rug all your flags in the same way.

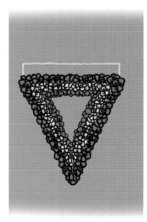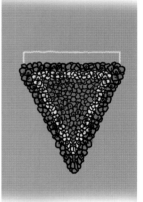

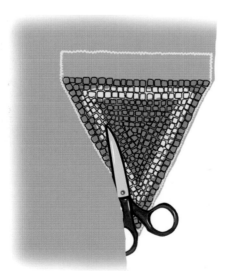

8 Trim off the excess burlap by cutting closely around the edge of the hemming, taking care not to cut the rag rug loops or stitches as you do so. You will be left with a rag rugged triangle and a bare tab at the top of the flag—do not cut this tab off.

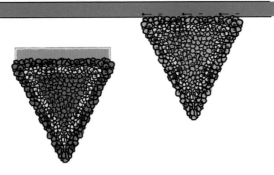

9 Lay the ribbon out flat and space the flags along it, about 2¾ in (7cm) apart and right side up. Remember to leave enough blank ribbon at each end to hang the bunting. Pin the bottom edge of the ribbon to the tab of each flag, as close to the rag rugging as possible.

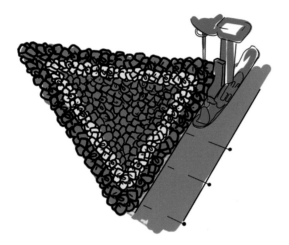

10 Thread the sewing machine to match the color of the ribbon. Attach the zipper foot if you have one (this allows you to sew closer to the rag rugging). Removing the pins as you go, sew the top of the ribbon to the tabs, stitching as close to the rag rugging as possible.

11 To hide the tabs, fold the ribbon over the burlap to enclose it. You may need to fold the burlap over on itself to make it narrow enough to be covered. Do this from one end of the ribbon to the other. Pin in place. Starting at one end of the ribbon, machine stitch along the line you have just pinned so that the burlap is no longer visible.

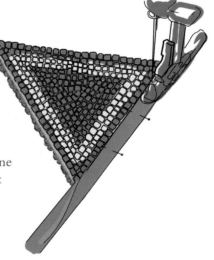

CELEBRATION STREAMER

Rag streamers are a very easy and inexpensive way to add handmade charm to any occasion. They look fabulous at celebrations (weddings, birthdays, and baby showers, for example), but can even add a little pizazz to your everyday life. I love the one I have draped across the end of my bed and my friend has one above her desk. The colors can be chosen to suit your taste and changing the lengths of the rags transforms the feel of the streamer—the longer they are, the more ethereal and "Midsummer Night's Dream" they look!

YOU WILL NEED

19½ ft (6 m) twine (I used 4-ply cotton baker's twine)—this will make a streamer with a finished length of 6½ ft (2 m)

2 chairs

Assorted fabrics (see tip)

Fabric scissors

COLOR PALETTE

Pastel blue, yellow, cream

TIP

USE LACE, SILK, AND CHIFFON FOR A BEAUTIFUL WEDDING STREAMER.

1 Cut the twine into three equal lengths and knot them together at one end. Braid/plait the lengths of twine together and tie in a knot at the other end (this makes the twine stronger).

2 Tie each end of the braid into a loop, so that your streamer can be hung easily once it is constructed. You can cut off the excess twine if you wish or leave it as a cute tassel.

3 Hook each loop around the top of a chair, so that the braid is suspended between the two chairs. It should be fairly taut. Make sure to weigh down the chairs with something heavy so that they do not tip over when the rags are tied on.

4 Prepare your fabric by cutting it into strips that are as long as possible (see pages 13–15). Cut the ends of the strips so that they are flat.

5 Take the first fabric strip and knot the center of the strip onto the braided twine so that both ends of the strip hang down. Continue knotting the fabric strips randomly along the twine until you are happy with the quantity of that particular fabric. Repeat until the streamer looks full, alternating fabrics and/or colors as you wish. Leave about 8 in (20 cm) at each end of the twine clear so that the streamer can be hung up easily.

SPRING WREATH

Spring is my favorite season of the year. After a long, cold winter, there are few things that are more beautiful or that bring more hope than seeing the first spring flowers poking their heads up through the soil. The colors in this wreath are a celebration of the first spring flowers that pop up in my garden—snowdrops, daffodils, iris, and grape hyacinths.

1 Follow steps 1–3 of the Festive Wreath instructions on pages 104–106.

YOU WILL NEED

Template on page 126

¼-in (5-mm) thick foamboard (or cardboard—see tip)

Marker pen

Cutting mat

Scalpel

Burlap/hessian

Sewing machine and thread

Assorted fabrics

Fabric scissors

Gauge

Latch hook

Everyday scissors

Staple gun

Burlap/hessian strands or ribbon, for hanging (optional)

Felt (optional)

Glue gun (optional)

COLOR PALETTE

Pale yellow, white, lilac, pastel pink, pastel blue, light and dark green

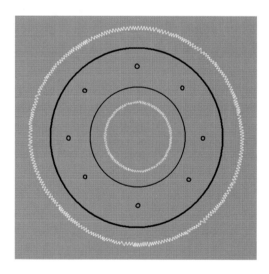

2 Use the marker pen to draw eight small circles inside the ring, equidistant from each other. These will become the centers of the flowers on your wreath. Don't worry about being too exact in your measurement, as rag rugging is a very forgiving craft and it won't show if your flowers aren't exactly the same distance apart.

TIP

IF YOU DO NOT HAVE FOAMBOARD, THICK CARDBOARD OR LAYERS OF CARDBOARD CAN BE USED AS AN ALTERNATIVE. THE CARDBOARD OR LAYERS MUST BE AT LEAST ¼ IN (5 MM) THICK OR THE WREATH WILL NOT HOLD ITS SHAPE.

3 Choose the fabric for the flower centers and cut into short pieces for shaggy rag rugging (see pages 13–15). Here I have mixed pale yellow fabric with white fabric, as an ode to the snowdrop! Tightly shaggy rag rug (see pages 21–22) four pieces into the center of each of the eight circles.

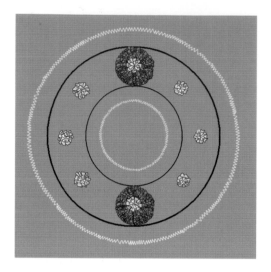

4 Choose two shades of pastel pink fabric and cut into short pieces. Mix the fabrics together in a pile and randomly shaggy rag rug in concentric rings around the first flower center until the top and bottom of the flower reach the edges of the ring. Try to mix the two shades well. Using the same pink fabrics, repeat on the circle opposite your first flower. You should now have two complete pink flowers.

5 Using two shades of each color, shaggy rag rug the flowers in pairs until all the flowers are fully rag rugged.

6 Shaggy rag rug in the areas between the flowers with pale and dark green to create "foliage." Continue until the wreath is fully rag rugged. If the flowers look a little squashed, remove some of the fabric strips around them to give them space to spread out.

7 Follow steps 6–9 of the Festive Wreath on pages 106–107 to assemble your spring wreath.

"LOVE YOU" HEART

Rag rug hearts make fun decorations for the home, as well as being unique wedding and Valentine's Day gifts. They look great hung on doors as well as perched on shelves and mantelpieces. I started out making the hearts in a variety of shades of red and pink, but soon started experimenting with different colors—I even did a rainbow one! So, don't be afraid to think outside the box and experiment with the colors you (or your giftee) love.

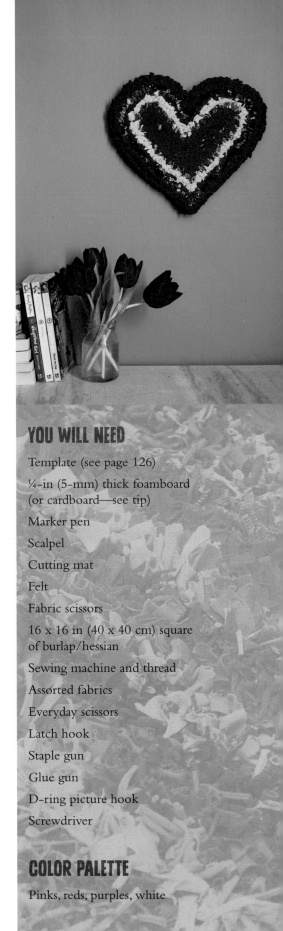

1 Copy the template on page 126, Place it on the foamboard and draw around it using the marker pen. Carefully cut out the heart shape using the scalpel. Make sure you do this on a cutting mat to protect your work surface.

2 Place the foamboard heart on the piece of felt. Draw around it with the marker pen, then cut out the heart. Put this aside for later use.

3 Place the foamboard heart on the burlap/hessian, allowing at least 2 in (5 cm) of burlap around each edge of the heart. Draw around the heart with the marker pen.

YOU WILL NEED

Template (see page 126)

¼-in (5-mm) thick foamboard (or cardboard—see tip)

Marker pen

Scalpel

Cutting mat

Felt

Fabric scissors

16 x 16 in (40 x 40 cm) square of burlap/hessian

Sewing machine and thread

Assorted fabrics

Everyday scissors

Latch hook

Staple gun

Glue gun

D-ring picture hook

Screwdriver

COLOR PALETTE

Pinks, reds, purples, white

TIP

IF YOU DO NOT HAVE FOAMBOARD, THICK CARDBOARD (OR LAYERS OF CARDBOARD GLUED TOGETHER) CAN BE USED AS AN ALTERNATIVE. THE CARDBOARD OR LAYERS MUST BE AT LEAST ¼ IN (5 MM) THICK OR THE HEART WILL NOT HOLD ITS SHAPE.

4 Sketch a second line on the burlap 1½ in (4 cm) outside the template line. Machine stitch along both heart outlines using placeholder hemming stitch (see page 13). This will hold the burlap in place. Cut off any loose threads.

5 Prepare the fabric by cutting it into long strips for loopy rag rugging (see pages 13–14). Your strips should be around ⅝ in (1.5cm) in width.

6 Loopy rag rug (see pages 18–19) the first row just outside the inner hemming. This will cover the sides of the heart so that none of the burlap will be visible when the heart is assembled. The loops should be approximately ⅝ in (1.5 cm) in height.

7 Use the same fabric to rag rug a second row just inside the inner hemming, keeping as close to the line of machine stitching as possible.

8 Continue rag rugging one row at a time in different shades of your chosen color until you reach the center of the heart and all the burlap is covered.

9 Trim the excess burlap from around the completed heart, making sure not to snip any of the stitching. This is best done using everyday scissors from the back of the burlap.

10 Place the rag rugged heart face down and align the foamboard with the rag rugging. Wrap the burlap border of the heart around and attach to the back of the foamboard using the staple gun. You will need to make a short cut in the burlap at the top of the heart and concertina the burlap around the edges to secure it in place.

TIP

YOU CAN KEEP SOME OF THE EXCESS BURLAP CUT AWAY IN STEP 9 TO USE FOR SMALLER PROJECTS, SUCH AS THE CHRISTMAS BAUBLES ON PAGE 108.

11 To tidy the back of the foamboard, attach the felt heart using the glue gun. Using a screwdriver, add a D-ring picture hook to the center of the back so that the heart can be hung.

TEMPLATES

Some templates are shown at their actual size, which means you can simply trace or photocopy them. Others are reduced in size, which means enlarging them on a photocopier For the Ammonite Rug, the Folk Art Wall Hanging, and the Ragged Life Letters, you will need to scale up the designs using grid paper (available online or from sewing stores).

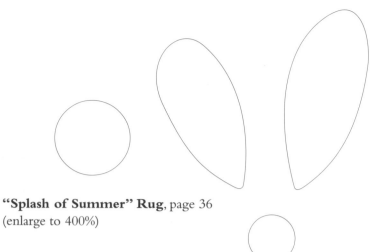

"Splash of Summer" Rug, page 36
(enlarge to 400%)

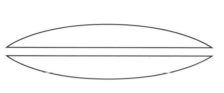

Iznik Rug, page 44
(enlarge to 400%)

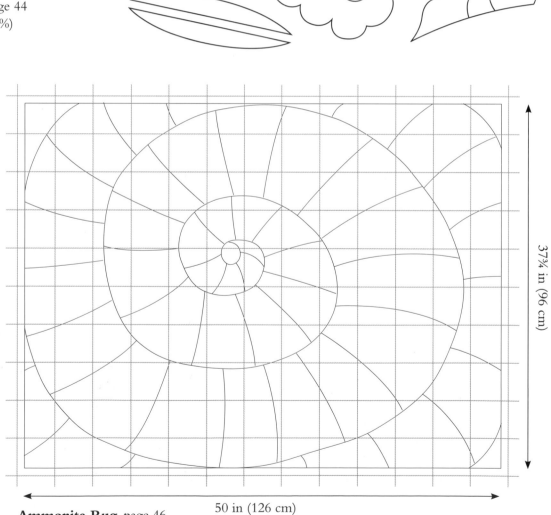

37¾ in (96 cm)

50 in (126 cm)

Ammonite Rug, page 46
Each square on the grid represents 4 in (10 cm)

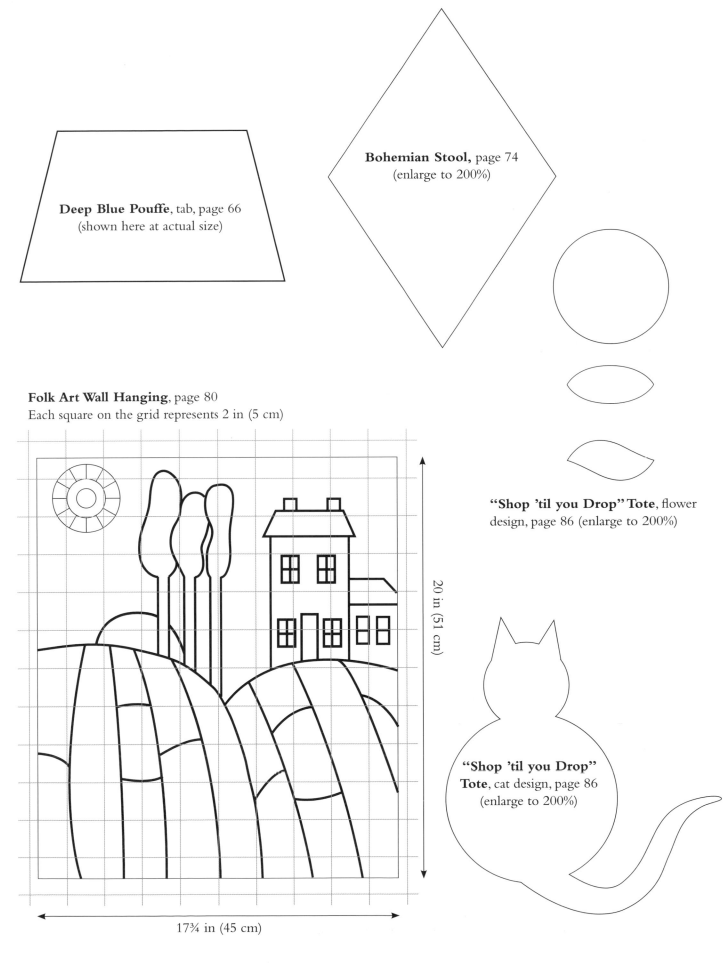

Deep Blue Pouffe, tab, page 66
(shown here at actual size)

Bohemian Stool, page 74
(enlarge to 200%)

Folk Art Wall Hanging, page 80
Each square on the grid represents 2 in (5 cm)

20 in (51 cm)

17¾ in (45 cm)

"Shop 'til you Drop" Tote, flower
design, page 86 (enlarge to 200%)

**"Shop 'til you Drop"
Tote**, cat design, page 86
(enlarge to 200%)

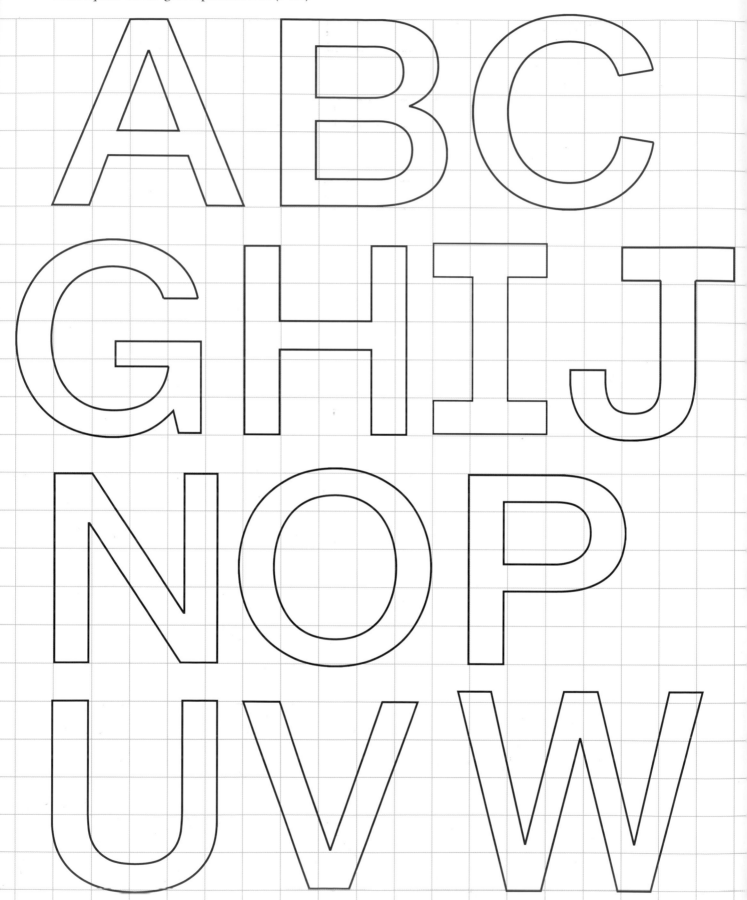

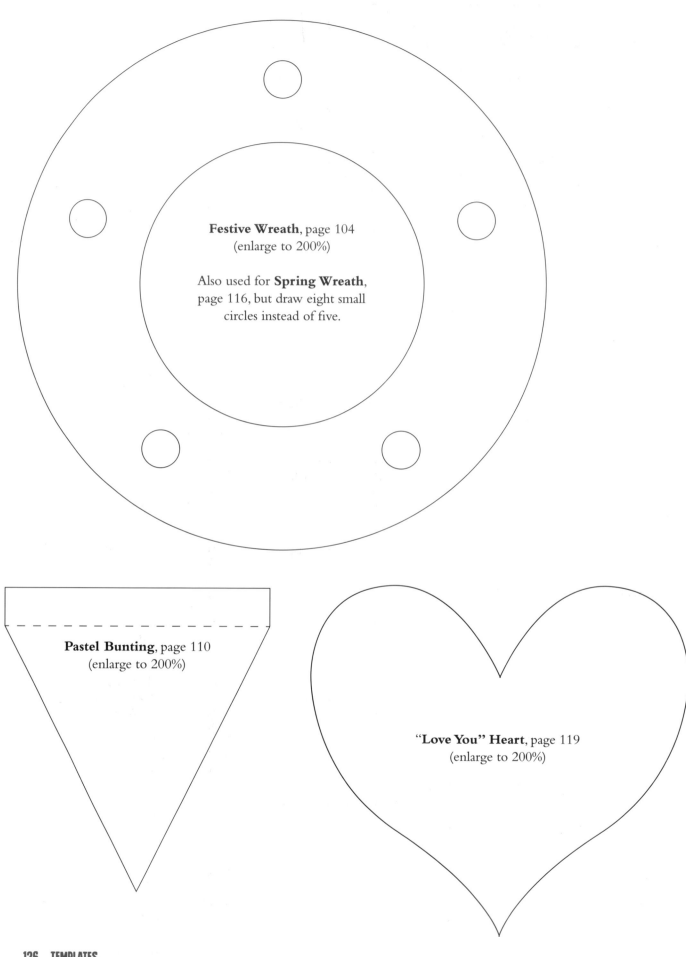

Festive Wreath, page 104
(enlarge to 200%)

Also used for **Spring Wreath**,
page 116, but draw eight small
circles instead of five.

Pastel Bunting, page 110
(enlarge to 200%)

"Love You" Heart, page 119
(enlarge to 200%)

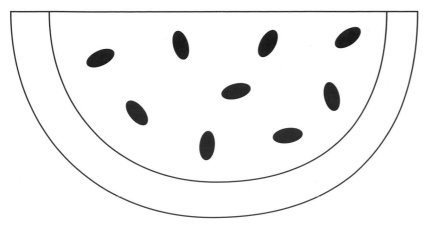

Watermelon Clutch, page 90 (enlarge to 200%)

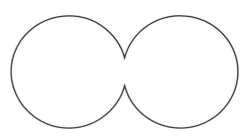

Christmas Tree Baubles, page 108
(shown here at actual size)

SUPPLIERS

Ragged Life
On my Ragged Life website you can buy all the rag rug tools used in the projects in this book or book yourself onto a rag rug workshop.
I ship globally.
+44 (0)7815 796285
www.ragged-life.com

eBay
A useful place to buy vintage rag rug tools. If you are looking to buy a rag rug spring tool, I recommend searching for a "Brown's Patent Rag Rug Tool" on eBay before buying a new one. The narrower point on Brown's Spring Tool makes for easier rag rugging.
www.ebay.com
www.ebay.co.uk

Etsy
A great place to see other crafters' rag rug designs and track down hard-to-find equipment.
www.etsy.com
www.etsy.com/uk

US
Hobby Lobby
Stores nationwide. Stocks the basic rag rug tools.
www.hobbylobby.com

Jo-Ann Fabric and Craft Stores
Stores nationwide. Pick up latch hooks and rug canvas here.
www.joann.com

Michaels
Stores nationwide. Lots of burlap options.
www.michaels.com

The Woolery
Stocks a lot of the basic rag rug equipment.
www.woolery.com

Halcyon Yarn
Nice for rug making inspiration.
www.halcyonyarn.com

UK
Iriss
Rag rug and other craft equipment.
66 Chapel Street
Penzance
Cornwall TR18 4AD
01736 366568
www.iriss.co.uk

The Threshing Barn
A great website for tools, workshops, and inspiration.
Unit 3, Mill 2
Farfield Mill
Garsdale Road
Sedbergh
Cumbria LA10 5LW
01539 620474
www.threshingbarn.com

Rag Art Studios
Great for tools and workshops.
Trefenter
LLanddewi Brefi
Tregaron
Ceredigion SY25 6SB
01974 298100
www.ragartstudios.com

Fred Aldous
Lovely independent shop with everything crafty, including rag rug equipment. Also sells online.
37 Lever Street
Manchester M1 1LW
0161 236 4224
www.fredaldous.co.uk

Hobbycraft
Stores nationwide.
0330 026 1400
www.hobbycraft.co.uk

John Lewis
Stores nationwide.
03456 049049
www.johnlewis.com

INDEX

ACKNOWLEDGMENTS

Thank you to my wonderfully creative family for immersing me in a world of art, craft, and beauty all my life. This book is dedicated to the original rag rug guru—my quirky but cool mum, Victoria. You taught me everything I know and this book is as much yours as it is mine. Lots of love to my dad, David, for spurring me on at all the right times, and my big brother, Ross, for keeping me grounded. Christian… where do I even start? You've been my rock from the very beginning—I love you. I'd also like to thank my rag-tag bunch of friends, in particular Kate, Kellie, and Stuart, for supporting me, believing in me, and tearing me away from my proofs when I needed it. You guys are the best. Aaron, Anil, Nigel, and James, thank you so much for all your hard work on Ragged Life over the past couple of years. It goes without saying, but you guys are great at what you do.

Thanks to the amazing team at CICO Books for making my first book a reality. Cheers to my lovely editor, Gillian, for working late nights and weekends to expertly edit all my rag rug ramblings. Thank you, Miriam, for project managing the entire process with such grace and apparent ease. Thanks Sally and Geoff for your beautiful designing and Harriet for your lovely illustrations. Finally, thank you to Cindy for tracking me down to write this book in the first place and to Penny for putting the wheels in motion. I couldn't have asked for a nicer and more talented team to work with.

And last, but not least, thank you to anyone who has ever taken one of my workshops, bought one of my pieces, or simply donated clothing to the rag rug cause. Your support of Ragged Life means the world to me.